AMERICAN COUNTRY LIVING

CANNING *and* PRESERVING

TECHNIQUES, RECIPES, USES, AND MORE

LINDA FERRARI

CRESCENT BOOKS

New York

A FRIEDMAN GROUP BOOK
This 1991 edition published by Crescent Books,
distributed by Outlet Book Company Inc., a Random House Company
225 Park Avenue South
New York, New York 10003

ISBN 0-517-69125-6

AMERICAN COUNTRY LIVING: CANNING AND PRESERVING
Techniques, Recipes, Uses, and More
was prepared and produced by Michael Friedman Publishing Group, Inc.
15 West 26th Street
New York, New York 10010

Editor: Sharon Kalman
Art Director: Jeff Batzli
Designer: Robert W. Kosturko
Photography Researcher: Daniella Jo Nilva

Typeset by M&M Typographers, Inc.
Color separation by Universal Colour Scanning Ltd.
Printed and bound in Hong Kong by Leefung-Asco Printers Ltd.

8 7 6 5 4 3 2

DEDICATION

For my Dad, who would have loved to have been a part of this. For all the love and encouragement he gave to me during his life. For his telling me I could do anything I had a notion to, and giving me the courage to try new things all the time. I love you Dad and miss you terribly.

ACKNOWLEDGMENTS

I want to thank my wonderful husband, Phil, who gave me encouragement all the way and cleaned up my terrible messes after I experimented with new recipes all day. And thanks to my mom, Evelyn Walker, who stood by me with such enthusiasm through this project. To my six wonderful children who have not complained about having jams and preserves three times a day because mommy did not have time to cook anything else. A special thanks to Dr. George York, the food technologist at University of California at Davis, and to his assistant, Kathryn Boor, who were both so helpful and so patient with my many calls. Thanks also to the people at Cuisinart and Williams-Sonoma for lending me some wonderful equipment. And to Sharon Kalman, my editor, for having the trust in me to do this project. And finally to my friend, Georgia Bockoven, who said I could do it and showed me the way.

CONTENTS

INTRODUCTION

THE HISTORY
OF CANNING
Page 8

CHAPTER ONE

CANNING BASICS
Page 12

CHAPTER TWO

CANNING FRUITS
AND TOMATOES
Page 22

CHAPTER THREE

JAMS, JELLIES,
AND PRESERVES
Page 54

CHAPTER FOUR

CANNING VEGETABLES
Page 82

CHAPTER FIVE

PICKLES, RELISHES,
AND CHUTNEYS
Page 94

CHAPTER SIX

VINEGARS, OILS,
AND OTHER GOODIES
Page 108

CHAPTER SEVEN

GIFTS FROM
THE KITCHEN
Page 118

SHOPPING GUIDE
Page 125

INDEX
Page 126

INTRODUCTION

THE HISTORY OF CANNING

Throughout history people have tried to think of ways to preserve their food. When they killed large animals, they tried smoking and drying the meat in hopes of preserving it for times when they were not so lucky or game was not so plentiful.

The turning point came in 1795 when the French army offered money to anyone who could discover a way to preserve food for their troops. Times were hard and even though the French were winning battles they were losing their troops to illness and malnutrition. The challenge was accepted by a Frenchman, Nicolas Appert, a chef and scientist who had experimented with preserving foods for many years. He laid out the first principles for food processing and preserving, using heat and closed containers. While Appert's means and lab equipment were meager, he was very organized and scientific in his approach.

Appert filled glass jars with food, corked the jars, and then wired them shut. He was aware that air had to be eliminated from the food to preserve it, but he did not fully understand why this was so important. He put the jars into sacks for cooking. This allowed him to safely lower the jars that may otherwise have broken during the cooking period.

In 1809, after years of tremendous effort and perseverance, Appert won the prize given by the French army for preserving food by heating a hermetically sealed container.

While a few other people had accomplished the feat of preserving food before Appert, he was the first person to apply his principles of preservation on a commercial level. He actually started a commercial cannery but saw it destroyed during the Napoleonic Wars. We are fortunate that Appert went on to write a paper detailing his discoveries.

Today, we are all beneficiaries of his knowledge and still use many of his principles.

Louis Pasteur, the great French scientist, helped us understand how Appert's concept of heat and the elimination of air helped destroy microorganisms that cause the decomposition of foods. Pasteur went on to teach the process of sterilization called pasturization. All of Pasteur's work was made easier by his use of the discoveries Appert had made.

Two other scientists, Samuel Prescott and William Underwood, studied the fundamental principles of bacteriology and their application to the canning process. Their most significant contribution was to let us realize just how important it is to carefully follow specific steps for the safety of our foods.

The final inventions fundamental to canning and preserving were the metal can by Peter Durand in 1810, the glass jar with threaded tops by John Mason in 1858, and the pressure canner by A. K. Shriver in 1874.

The metal can underwent continuous improvements to reach its present state of development, eliminating rusting, which was a serious problem. The last mechanical improvement in canning was the invention of the metal lid for glass jars. This device helped to prolong the life of the preserved food.

All of this knowledge came from the desire to solve a single common problem: The need to have foods available to everyone, everywhere, throughout the year. We have taken the process to such lengths that we now have freeze-dried foods for campers and astronauts. Today, more and more people are taking up canning simply for the pure pleasure it offers, to give as special gifts, and the beauty of having our summer pleasures packed into a jar year round.

CHAPTER ONE

CANNING BASICS

There are many reasons people today are returning to the crafts of yesteryear. Quilting, basket weaving, doll making, rug braiding, and canning are just a few of the things our ancestors did. They canned to make a harvest last from one season to another. They made quilts to keep their families warm. They made baskets to carry laundry, fruit, groceries, even children. They wove rugs so they would have something on their floors.

Today we do these things to recall old times, or because we take pride in doing something for ourselves in a world where anything desired can be bought. We think of many of these crafts as a form of art because of the skill they require. I like to can because I take pride in the fact that I can give my family and friends wonderful summer flavors all year long. I love to cook and use my canned goods in many intriguing ways. I can also give my best friend her favorite summertime fruit at Christmas, and it tastes just as fresh as if it was just picked.

APPROPRIATE FOODS FOR CANNING

The secret to having nice, fresh-tasting fruits and vegetables is starting out with fresh, firm, ripe fruits and vegetables. Most of us don't have an orchard in our backyard and that's why it is a good idea to look for places in your area to buy fresh produce. Remember, as soon as fruits and vegetables are picked they begin to deteriorate. There are farmers in almost every town who bring their produce into the city to sell at either indoor or outdoor farmers' markets. You can buy from trucks on the roadsides, or look for produce terminals or canneries who will sell to people who are willing to buy large quantities. They will sell by the lug, bushel, crate, or box; buying in bulk helps to lower your price.

I am lucky enough to live in an area devoted to fruit growing. There is a place nearby called Apple Hill, which consists of several farms that band together at different times of the year to sell different fruits. For example, in the early summer they sell several varieties of cherries. You can buy by the lug or box if you want. They have desserts made from cherries, and one farm even had a cherry pit spitting contest. At apple time, the farms sell all varieties of apples as well as apple pies, fritters, jams, cider, and even apple dolls. Some of the farms have craft fairs and one even has fishing for the kids and helicopter rides for those with strong stomachs. There are many ways to get your fruit and some are really fun.

If you have a small garden and a few fruit trees, you know that sometimes you have more than enough food to can at home. You may also preserve on the same day for real freshness.

Once you have found a place to buy your produce and know that it must be firm, crisp, and ripe, you want to make sure that you protect the beautiful color of your canned foods. Simply cut the food directly into a gallon of water into which you have added 2 tablespoons each of vinegar and salt. This will give a slight flavor to your food so make sure that you thoroughly rinse it before adding the canning liquid. You could also use a commercial powdered ascorbic acid solution that is added to water, being careful to follow directions on the package.

CANNING EQUIPMENT

Starting off with the proper equipment will make canning easier and safer. Some of the equipment is absolutely essential for the safety and quality of successfully canned foods. Other equipment listed here is very helpful and makes your job easier. You probably have most of the equipment you will need for canning, but if you do not you can purchase

it at most grocery or hardware stores. For hard to find equipment or specialty equipment look at the mail order sources in the back of the book.

CANNING JARS AND LIDS: Canning jars are made of high-tempered glass to withstand the changing temperatures that occur in the canning process. Because of the temperature changes, it is not recommended that you ever use commercial jars that were used for mayonnaise, jelly, or other store-bought foods. These jars could easily crack during processing.

Canning jars come with wide-mouth or regular mouth openings. The wide-mouth variety is much easier to use for fruits and vegetables. The regular mouth jars are great for jams, jellies, and preserves.

Jars come in many sizes: ½-pint, pint, 1½-pint (12-ounce), and quart. Choose the size that is most convenient for what you are preparing.

The most common lid is flat, metal, and self seals with a metal screw band. The flat metal lid can only be used once, but you can use the metal screw bands over and over again. Discard metal screw bands if they have become rusty or are bent out of shape.

Make sure you always check your jars before canning, discarding any that are cracked or nicked.

Decorative jars that have wire bails and rubber rings are very tricky to use when processing foods. For one thing, most of the decorative jars with clamp tops are not made of glass strong enough to withstand the heat required to process the food. When you fill the jars with food and liquid you then place the rubber ring (a new one each time you use the jar) around the lid, close the jar and catch the small wire loop on the lid to the clamp. You only catch the lid because if you totally lock it at this stage the seal is too tight and it may explode during the heating process. On most of these jars just "catching the lid" is not a very tight fit, so during processing water can leak into your food. These jars are very pretty and are much better used with jams, jellies, preserves, marmalades, and butters, where processing will not involve the risk of spoilage.

If, however, you have older jars (with the glass dome lids), then you are in luck because the loop of the bail holds the top down tight enough for a good seal before processing in water. Be careful to check these jars carefully for chips on the glass and rust on the bails because of their age.

Always wash the jars in hot soapy water and rinse well. Wash and rinse the metal bands also. The metal lids with sealing compound should be put in boiling water a few minutes before putting on the jar for proper sealing. Follow the manufacturer's directions found on your package of lids. If you use rubber rings, use new, clean rings each time; wash them in hot soapy water and rinse before use, being careful not to stretch the rubber rings.

CANNERS: There are basically three kinds of canners: the water bath canner, the pressure canner, and the steam canner.

The water bath canner is used for fruit, tomatoes, butters, pickles, relishes, and anything else high in acid. You can buy the distinctive, large, black-spotted water bath canners in almost any grocery or hardware store. They come with a rack that holds and separates seven jars of food. You can also use any lightweight pot that is at least 12 inches deep and has a lid. In this case you will have to place a rack in the pan to keep the jars from touching the bottom of the pan and to let the air circulate properly. The canner should be at least 4 inches taller than the jars, because you need at least 2 inches of water above the jars plus boiling room. Remember the water bath canner is used only for high-acid foods. The recipes in this book will specify which canning procedure to use for which recipe.

The second canning process is pressure canning. This is used when processing low-acid foods such as vegetables, meat, fish, and poultry. The pressure canner is the only way for us to get heat high enough to insure the safety of low-acid foods. There are many brands of pressure canners, but as they are sometimes hard to find I have given some suggestions where to find them in the mail-order section of this book. A pressure canner is a metal kettle and cover that are clamped together to make them steam tight. There is a weight gauge that usually reads 5, 10, and 15 pounds, plus a vent or petcock, and a pressure safety valve.

On some pressure canners there will also be a dial pressure gauge. Make sure you always carefully follow the instructions that come with your pressure canner. For the safe operation of your pressure canner always make sure your safety valve opening and petcock are clean. Hold it up and look through the safety valve opening to see if you can see through it. If you can't, run a string through it and clean it. Do this often during the canning season.

Last, we have steam canning. It can be used instead of a water bath canner for acid foods such as tomatoes, fruits, and pickles. This is *not* a pressure canner. The food is processed by a flow of steam instead of being submerged in water. You can use the same time schedules that you use with a water bath canner. Most experts on canning prefer water bath canning to this method and consider water bath canning to be safer.

COLANDERS and STRAINERS: These are a necessity when cleaning fruits and vegetables. A strainer is also very handy when making jellies. You can put a piece of cheesecloth in a strainer and strain the fruit juices until they are clear. If you do not have a food processor or food mill you can force fruits through a strainer for butters and sauces.

WIDE MOUTH CANNING FUNNELS: Wide and small mouth funnels are used to keep the rims of the jars clean. The wide mouth funnel will fit into the canning jar and the small size is great for funneling syrups or vinegars into fancy or decorative bottles.

JAR LIFTER: This device has rubber on its ends and makes lifting hot jars out of boiling water much safer.

LABELS: Labels are very handy, not only as a reminder of what is inside the jar, but also the date it was canned.

LADLES: Ladles are necessary because they make it easy and less messy to pour syrups or hot cooking liquids over the prepared foods. You will have fewer spills or drips, leaving your jars cleaner.

LARGE BOWLS: You will need these to hold fruit, to acidify vegetables, and to use in making freezer jams. Actually, you will find that you use them in hundreds of ways while canning.

LARGE POTS AND PANS: These are needed for precooking foods and to make jams and jellies. Large sizes (6 to 10 quarts) are best and allow for boiling room. I also have a large unlined copper pan for making my jellies and I love it; of course, this is not a necessity. The best pots to use are the nonreactive kind that will not discolor or change the flavor of the food. Heavy weight stainless or heavy enamel is probably your best bet.

LONG HANDLED SPOONS and SLOTTED SPOONS: Use these to stir boiling substances without burning your hands. Slotted spoons are particularly useful to remove parboiled fruits and vegetables from boiling liquid.

MEASURING CUPS and SPOONS: These are absolutely necessary for accurate measuring. One- to four-cup measures are essential, and a one-quart measuring cup is very useful.

SHARP KNIVES: A sharp knife is very important for preparing food. In my opinion, stainless steel is the best because it will not discolor the food.

THERMOMETER: This is necessary in measuring the jell point of jams and jellies. When the jelly reaches a temperature of 220°F the jelly is ready. This temperature is for sea level. If you are not at sea level boil some water and see what the temperature is when it boils and add 8°F to that and you will have your jell point.

TIMER: It is absolutely essential to assure that directions are followed accurately. You want to prevent possible spoilage and assure the right jell to your jams and jellies.

VEGETABLE BRUSH: A vegetable brush is a good way to assure that your fruits and vegetables are clean.

EQUIPMENT THAT IS HELPFUL

Apple Corer and Peeler: This is a great gadget and prepares apples quickly for canning, cooking, and making pies.

Cheesecloth: This is helpful in straining jellies and juices.

Cherry Pitter: This simple device makes an easy job of getting your cherries ready for canning, either in syrup or in brandy. The cherries look beautiful when canned and it is nice not to have to worry about the pits when you eat them. Williams-Sonoma sells a really nice one that makes less mess than most. It is the Leifheit Cherrymat.

Food Mill: This is a handheld tool that purees the juice and pulp of fruits and vegetables. This is great for fruit butters, applesauce, and all sorts of sauces. It separates the puree from the seeds and skin.

Food Processor: This is one of my favorite tools for any type of cooking. I find it extremely helpful with canning. It chops and cuts vegetables in beautiful, even pieces and purees fruits for jams and jellies. Cuisinart makes a strainer attachment for their processor that is wonderful. It strains so well that you can actually put raspberries in it and produce a beautiful, clear juice perfect for jelly, with no seeds at all. It also makes a great applesauce by separating the pulp from the skin and seeds. You can even make fruit, vegetable, and meat baby foods with this attachment.

Jelly Bag: A mesh bag suspended by a metal holder to hold cooked or mashed fruit, allowing the juices to drain.

Tongs: These are useful for removing lids from hot water and placing them on the jars, and for arranging foods inside jars that are hard to reach.

Towels: You need towels to wipe the rims of your jars; they are also useful as a safe place to put hot jars.

Courtesy Ball Jar Corporation

PREPARATION METHODS

COLD or RAW PACK METHOD: With this method you clean, cut, and prepare raw fresh fruits or uncooked vegetables and put the food into hot, sterilized jars. Boiling liquid or syrup is then poured into the jars. Continue by releasing the air bubbles, cleaning the rims, and sealing the jars. Process according to directions.

HOT PACK: Prepare the fruit or vegetables and partially cook them, then pack them hot into hot, sterilized jars and cover with hot liquid or syrup. You can use the same liquid you used to cook the food in. Release the air and add more liquid if necessary; seal and process.

OPEN KETTLE METHOD: This is used for jams, jellies, preserves, conserves, marmalades, and butters. First cook the food to the jell point (which is 8°F above the temperature at which water boils), then pour the boiling hot food into hot, sterilized jars and seal. The food does not necessarily need to be further processed; however, I like to process my fruit preserves for 10 minutes in a hot water bath to assure a good seal. You must never use this method on vegetables or meats as microorganisms will assuredly grow and cause contamination.

OVEN CANNING METHOD: This is a process that you may remember your mother or grandmother using. *This method is not recommended as the foods simply do not get hot enough to kill microorganisms.* With heat distribution being so uneven and the likely possibility of jars exploding upon removal from the oven, it is best to use another canning method.

MICROWAVE CANNING: This is a rather new process for those who don't want to can large amounts of food. If you have a small garden with a small yield then this is a great way to can as your produce becomes ripe.

MICROWAVE CANNING

Though I am an avid canner, microwave canning has never been my choice. If my tree is brimming with fruit or I have bought several lugs of fruit, I would want to can it all within a few days. However, I can understand how someone with a small garden or a few baskets of fruit really wouldn't want to get out all the equipment to can so little. For these circumstances microwave canning may be for you.

You must still always sterilize your canning jars and lids. You will also have to process your jams and jellies in a water bath, freeze or refrigerate them, or use paraffin to seal them. If you decide to use paraffin, you have to melt it on the top of a double boiler, since paraffin will not melt in a microwave oven, as the microwaves go straight through it.

There is a product that has been out on the market for a couple of years now, called the MICRO-DOME. The MICRO-DOME is a small pressure canner that holds one pint jar or one half-pint jar at a time. When you buy the MICRO-DOME it comes with a booklet full of recipes. They advise you to only use the recipes that have been specially designed to be used in the MICRO-DOME.

To give you an example, if you are canning fresh pineapple you would cut the pineapple and pack it into the jar tightly to extract its own juice. Seal the jar and microwave according to the directions given with the canner. You remove the canner when a little whistle sounds, then put it into a sink full of tepid water to let it cool. After it cools, remove it from the canner and let it cool again, then store it. The jar will lose some liquid during the canning process. However the MICRO-DOME people assure us that this is all right and that the product will still be safe. Make sure you read all the directions before using an appliance like this to insure the safety of the food you produce.

SEALING METHODS

LIDS and RINGS: The safest lid is a flat metal lid with a ring of sealer running around the inner edge of the lid. These are held on the jars with a metal screw band. You must heat the flat lid for 2 to 3 minutes in boiling water before applying it to the jar (see manufacturer's insert). The screw band is then screwed on tightly and the jar can be processed.

PARAFFIN: Paraffin can be bought in slabs in grocery or hardware stores. It is used to seal jams, jellies, preserves, marmalades, and fruit butters. You must be very careful when handling paraffin because it could burn you badly. Never melt it over direct heat. Instead, melt the paraffin in a double boiler, keeping it over hot water until ready to use. Cover jelly with ⅛ of an inch of paraffin and tilt the jar to make sure the paraffin touches all sides for a proper seal. If bubbles form you can pop them, but it is not necessary. If you ever have a paraffin fire just put a lid over it. *Never put water on a paraffin fire.*

FANCY CANNING JARS with BAIL LIDS: These jars are very pretty and successfully hold jams, jellies, preserves, and the like. However, if you try to put up foods that require processing you could run into trouble. To process you have to close the lid and push down the bail, but do not yet snap it into the lock position. While it is being processed water can easily seep into the jar. Do not totally lock the jar until processing is complete; unfortunately, by then water has seeped into your food. Remember, when using these jars you must always have a new rubber ring for proper sealing.

© Robert Edwards

COOLING, TESTING, AND STORING CANNED FOOD

Always remove jars from boiling water with a jar lifter, holding a folded cloth under the jar so no hot water drips on you. Let the jars cool on a wooden surface, on a wire rack, or on a folded towel. Separate the jars so air can circulate easily around them. When the jars are cool, test the seals by pressing the lids with your finger. The lids should not give and should have a slight concave appearance.

Foods that don't appear to be sealed properly can be reprocessed or refrigerated and used within a few days. You can remove the screw caps from the jars and store them until the next time you preserve. Store your canned goods in a dark, cool, dry place.

FOOD SPOILAGE

Microorganisms are present in all fresh foods. Acid helps to inhibit growth, but low-acid foods need the pressure canner to get the heat high enough to destroy microorganisms.

If you are very careful in following the procedures for canning in this book, it is unlikely that any of your canned food will spoil. But if, for some reason, the food was not processed long enough or not sealed properly there is a chance of spoilage. Spoiled canned food can cause a serious illness called botulism. Botulism is caused by the toxin produced by the growth of clostridium botulinum in low-acid foods or foods that have become low acid.

Botulism can be fatal and it is not easily detected. It has no smell. Never taste any canned food which shows gas pressure in the jar, that is mushy, moldy, or has a bad odor.

If you have any question about the food being spoiled, boil it for 30 minutes. Smell it while it is simmering. Any off odor is more detectable by boiling. The odor you should worry about is one that is rancid or somewhat putrid smelling. If there is any doubt about the contents of a jar, do not taste it. If someone has tasted spoiled food call a doctor immediately. It would be a good idea to take the food with you to the doctor's office touching the jar as little as possible and washing your hands with alcohol and water.

CHAPTER TWO

CANNING FRUITS AND TOMATOES

When summer comes we all love the wonderful fresh tastes of the fruits that become ripe during these months. If you have fruit trees, they are probably brimming with fruit and producing faster than you can eat it. Isn't it great that we are able to preserve these fruits? Even if you don't have your own garden, it is hard to resist the farmers' markets, roadside food vendors, or even the produce your market is displaying.

In this chapter I will not only give fruit recipes, but pie fillings and some great ideas for tomatoes.

You will love preserving all these wonderful tastes for your family and friends.

When canning fruit you must pick firm, ripe fruit that is free of blemishes. Fruit can be left whole, halved, or sliced. Smooth skinned fruit such as plums or cherries can be canned with the skin left on. Be sure to prick the skin before canning so it will not burst during cooking. Other fruits can be easily peeled by putting the whole fruit in boiling water for 30 seconds and then putting it into cold water. The skins will peel right off. This is also how to peel tomatoes for canning.

If sugar content is a concern of yours, it is good to know that all fruit can be canned without the addition of sugar. Syrup is added to make the fruit taste better and to hold the color. You can use the juice of the fruit, water, or commercial juice without sugar, filling the jar to within ½ inch of the top and process the same as if you used a sugar-based syrup.

All fruit and tomatoes are processed in a water bath canner because of the amount of acid in fruit. If the fruit is very ripe you may want to add a couple of tablespoons of bottled lemon juice to each quart of fruit to assure the amount of acid is correct.

STEP-BY-STEP PROCEDURES FOR CANNING FRUIT

CHECK AND CLEAN ALL EQUIPMENT: Check jars for nicks and cracks and make sure screw-on lids are rust-free and not bent. Wash all jars and screw lids in soapy water and sterilize by boiling them right side up on the rack in a boiling-water canner. Make sure you have new flat lids each time you can.

PREPARE FOOD FOR CANNING: Pick firm, ripe fruit or tomatoes, making sure it has no bruises or blemishes. Prepare just enough to fill the canner each time. Be sure to protect the fruit color with a commercial anti-darkening solution or ascorbic acid. Follow the package directions.

PICKING YOUR SYRUP OR LIQUID: You may can fruit in plain water, although sugar enhances the flavor in high-acid fruits. You can also flavor with artificial sweeteners, but I do not recommend this because they can become bitter with heating. You could, however, add the artificial sweetener right before serving and avoid the problem of bitterness. On pages 67 and 68 are recipes for low- and no-sugar fruits.

Sugar Syrups: light—2 cups sugar, 4 cups water
     medium—3 cups sugar, 4 cups water
     heavy—4¾ cups sugar, 4 cups water

Corn Syrup can replace the sugar or you can use a combination of corn syrup and sugar.

Honey can also replace sugar, but don't use a strong flavored honey as it will overpower the flavor of the fruit.

Fruit Juice can also cover the fruit. Commercially prepared juices or fresh juice from the fruit may be used. I like to can tomatoes in their own juice.

FILLING THE JARS
Raw Pack—Tightly pack your fruit into the jars and cover with the boiling liquid of your choice. Leave a ¼-inch headspace.

Hot Pack—Cook the fruit in the packing liquid for a few minutes before packing it in jars, leaving ½-inch headspace. Cover with boiling liquid and proceed.

REMOVING AIR BUBBLES: Use a plastic or rubber knife or spatula and insert on side of jar to release air bubbles. Add more liquid if necessary.

CLEANING THE RIMS OF THE JARS: Using a wet cloth, remove drips of syrup or liquid that might prevent the lid from sealing.

APPLYING THE LIDS: Follow the manufacturer's directions on the box—they usually recommend putting the lids in boiling water for 2 or 3 minutes to insure a proper seal. Screw on the metal bands immediately.

PROCESSING METHODS: All fruits are processed in a water bath canner. Make sure the water will be high enough to cover the jars by 2 inches and that the water has reached a full boil before adding the jars. Carefully lower the jars into the canner. Add boiling water, if necessary, to cover the jars. Cover the canner. When the water returns to a gentle boil, begin counting the processing time. At altitudes above 3,000 feet, add 2 minutes processing time for each additional 1,000 feet.

PROPER LIFTING OF THE JARS: Be very careful removing the jars from boiling water. Use a lifter made for this purpose and hold a folded cloth under the jar so hot liquid won't drop on you.

COOLING JARS: Allow the jars to cool on a wood surface, metal rack, or folded towels. A cold surface will crack the jars. Place jars in a draft-free spot with space between them to allow a free circulation of air.

CHECKING THE SEAL: There is no sweeter sound to a canner than the "pop" of the lid as it sits and cools. When you hear that pop you know that it has properly sealed. If, after the jars have cooled, the lid is not concave in appearance, test the seal by pressing on the lid with your finger. The lid should not move.

PROPER STORAGE: Label and date your jars and store them in a cool, dark place.

© Christopher Bain

© Dana White (both photos)

1. Picking out fresh, firm, ripe fruit and vegetables will assure the best flavor.

2. Check all jars for cracks and nicks. Check screw-on bands and discard any that are bent or rusty. Always start with new flat lids so you will be assured of a good seal. When you have determined which jars can be used, fill a kettle with water and bring it to a simmer.

STEP-BY-STEP PROCEDURE FOR CANNING TOMATOES

3. Wash jars and rings so that you are starting with clean equipment.

4. Wash your produce properly, ensuring that any traces of chemicals are gone.

© Dana White (both photos)

© Dana White (both photos)

5. Peel and seed any fruits and vegetables that may need it, preparing only enough food for one canner load at a time.

6. Prepare the produce by leaving it whole, slicing it, or dicing it. Always read your recipe beforehand so that you will know exactly how to prepare it. At this time you will also want to prepare the liquid or syrup you will be using and bring it to a boil.

7. Once your jars have been cleaned, hold them in a pan on top of the stove with 2 to 3 inches of simmering water until they are ready to use.

8. Place tomatoes in the jar with either a ladle and a funnel or by hand.

© Dana White (both photos)

9. When raw packing, make sure the jars are already hot (see step 7), then add boiling liquid. If the jars are not hot, the addition of the boiling liquid will make them shatter. Use a funnel to add hot liquid; this will help to keep the rims of the jars clean.

10. Always remove air bubbles and clean rims before applying the flat lids. Boil the flat lids for a couple of minutes, then apply them along with the screw bands.

11. Carefully set jars on a canning rack and slowly lower into simmering water.

12. If the water does not cover the jars by 2 inches, add simmering water to the kettle. Never pour cold water over the jars—this will cause them to break. Process, boiling gently for the recommended period of time.

13. Using a jar lifter with rubber ends, carefully remove the jars, using a folded cloth under the jar so hot water will not drip on you. Place on a towel or wooden surface to cool.

14. When the jars are cool, you can remove the ring bands and use them for future canning.

15. To test for a good seal, press on the lid with your finger. The lid should not move or make a sound.

16. Always label and date your jars. Place them in a dark, cool place.

SOME COMMON QUESTIONS ABOUT CANNING FRUIT AND TOMATOES

Why is liquid lost during the canning process and should it be replaced? Canning liquid is usually lost because of over-packing the jars. If this should happen it will not hurt the quality of the product, but the food above the liquid may darken. There is no need to replace the liquid—if you did you would have to reprocess the food or it will spoil.

Is it safe to eat the discolored food? The food should be fine. However, if there is an off odor to the food, discard it.

Do the black deposits on the underside of lids indicate spoilage? No, these deposits are harmless if the seal is good. Natural compounds in some foods corrode the metal.

Why do some fruits turn dark brown after being canned? Possibly you forgot to protect the color of the fruit while preparing it for processing. Once it turns color there is nothing you can do. It is a good idea to add a tablespoon or two of lemon juice per quart, or two teaspoons per pint, to each jar.

Why do some fruits float to the top of a jar? Fruits and tomatoes usually shrink when they are processed, so make sure you have packed the fruit tightly.

HOW TO PREPARE FRUIT FOR CANNING

FRUIT	HOW TO PREPARE	PROCESSING TIME	
		PINT	QUART
		minutes	
APPLES	Pare, cut in halves or quarters, and trim off core. To keep from darkening, dip in 1 gallon of water that contains 2 tablespoons each of salt and vinegar. Drain. Cook in hot syrup for 2 to 4 minutes according to the variety. Pack hot. Cover with hot liquid and seal.	15	15
APPLESAUCE	Wash, pare, if desired, quarter, and core cooking apples. Simmer, covered, in a small amount of water until tender. Press through sieve or food mill. Sweeten if desired. Reheat to boiling and pack into hot jars. Add 1 tablespoon lemon juice to top of each jar. Seal.	20	20
APRICOTS	Choose firm, well-colored apricots that are not overripe. To peel, dip in boiling water for 1 minute, then plunge into cold water and peel, or can apricots without peeling. Leave whole, or cut in halves and remove pits. **To pack hot:** Bring to a boil in liquid and just heat through or cook about 1 to 3 minutes. Pack hot and cover with hot liquid. Seal. **To pack raw:** Fill the jars with uncooked apricots. Cover with boiling liquid. Seal.	20 25	20 30
BERRIES OTHER THAN STRAWBERRIES	Drain well after washing. For firm berries, add ½ cup sugar to each quart of fruit. Cover pan, bring to a boil, and shake to keep fruit from sticking. Pack hot and cover with hot liquid. Seal. For red raspberries and other soft berries, fill jars with raw fruit and shake down for a full pack. Cover with boiling syrup made with juice or water (½ cup sugar and about ¾ cup juice for each quart). Seal.	10 10	10 15
CHERRIES	Wash, remove stems, sort for size and ripeness, and pit if desired. If left whole, prick to help prevent splitting. **To pack hot:** For pitted cherries, follow directions for firm berries. For cherries with pits, follow directions for firm berries but add a little water to prevent sticking or bring to a boil in hot syrup. Pack hot and seal. **To pack raw:** Pack into hot jars. Cover with boiling syrup or juice. Seal.	15 20	15 25
FIGS	Use tree-ripened figs that are not overripe. Sort and wash. Bring to a boil in hot water. Let stand in the hot water for 3 to 4 minutes. Drain. Pack hot into hot jars. Add 1 tablespoon of lemon juice to each 1-quart jar. Cover with boiling liquid. Do not use baking soda in preparing figs. Seal.	90	90
FRUIT JUICES	Wash, remove pits, if desired, and crush fruit. Heat to simmering to release juice. Strain through a cloth bag. Some fruits are not normally heated before extracting the juice. Fruits not heated are apples, white cherries, grapefruit, white grapes, lemons, and oranges. (Navel orange juice will be bitter and is not recommended for canning.) Sweeten juice to taste. Immediately heat or reheat juice to simmering. **To pack hot:** Fill hot jars with hot juice to ½ inch of top. Seal.	15	15

FRUIT	HOW TO PREPARE	PROCESSING TIME	
		PINT	QUART
		minutes	
GRAPEFRUIT	Use thoroughly ripened fruit. Peel. Separate segments and peel them. Pack segments in jars. Cover with hot syrup. Seal.	20	25
GRAPES	Use ripe Muscat or slightly underripe seedless grapes for canning. Remove stems and wash.		
	To pack hot: Bring to a boil in a small amount of liquid. Pack hot into hot jars. Cover with the hot liquid and seal.	15	15
	To pack raw: Put into hot jars and cover with boiling liquid. Seal.	20	20
NECTARINES	Follow directions for freestone peaches.		
NOPALES	Remove spines from young, tender cactus leaves. Cut into cubes or strips. Diced or cubed cactus is easier to handle, but either strips or cubes may be used. Rinse diced cactus once or twice in cold water. Place diced cactus in water, bring to a boil, and turn down to simmer. Cook until tender, about 10 to 15 minutes.		
	To pack hot: Pack hot into clean jars. Add ½ teaspoon salt and 1 teaspoon lemon juice or vinegar per pint; 1 teaspoon salt and 2 teaspoons lemon juice or vinegar per quart. Add other spices (garlic, cloves, or onion powder, for example) if desired. Cover with water leaving ½ inch headspace. Seal.	15	20
ORANGES	For Valencia or Mandarin oranges, follow directions for grapefruit. Other orange varieties are not recommended, because they become bitter.		
PEACHES	To peel all except canning varieties of clingstones, dip in boiling water for about 1 minute, plunge into cold water, then slip off skins. Cut into halves and remove pits. To keep from darkening, dip in 1 gallon of water that contains 2 tablespoons each of salt and vinegar. Drain at once. Peel canning varieties of clingstone peaches like you would apples, preferably with a stainless steel knife. Once peeled, a cut around the peach and a twisting motion between the hands will remove one-half of the fruit from the pit. You can remove the pit from the second half with a special spoon-shaped knife or cut it out carefully with a paring knife.		
	To pack hot: If fruit is juicy, add ½ cup sugar to each quart of raw fruit. Bring to a boil. Drop less juicy fruit into a medium-thin syrup that is boiling hot. Just heat through. Pack hot. Cover with boiling liquid. Seal.		
	Clingstone.	20	25
	Freestone.	15	20
	To pack raw: Pack in jars with the cut side down and the edges overlapping. Cover with boiling liquid. Seal.		
	Clingstone	25	30
	Freestone	20	25

University of California, Davis; Department of Food Technology.

FRUIT	HOW TO PREPARE	PROCESSING TIME	
		PINT	QUART
		minutes	
PEARS	Ripen pears for canning after picking. Do not allow them to become too soft. Pare, cut in halves, and trim out cores. **To pack hot:** Same as for less juicy peaches. Seal. **To pack raw:** Same as for peaches. Seal.	15 20	20 25
PINEAPPLE	Pare firm but ripe pineapple. Slice crosswise or cut into wedges. Remove the core and trim the "eye." Simmer pineapple in light syrup or pineapple juice until tender. **To pack hot:** Pack hot slices or wedges (spears) into hot jars. Cover with hot cooking liquid, leaving ½ inch headspace. Seal.	15	20
PLUMS AND FRESH PRUNES	Sort, remove stems, and wash. If canning whole, prick to help prevent bursting, or cut into halves. **To pack hot:** Bring to a boil in juice or in a thin to medium syrup. Pack hot. Cover with boiling liquid. Seal. **To pack raw:** Pack the fruit into the jar. Cover with boiling juice or syrup. Seal.	15 20	15 20
RHUBARB	Cut into ½-inch lengths. Add ½ cup sugar to each quart of rhubarb and let stand 3 to 4 hours to draw out juice. Bring to a boil. Pack hot. Cover with hot juice. Seal.	10	10
STRAWBERRIES	Not recommended because the product is usually not satisfactory.		
TOMATOES	Sort, picking out any that are spoiled or green. Do not can overripe tomatoes. They may be too low in acid for safe water bath canning. (If tomatoes are excessively dirty, wash with a solution containing 4 teaspoons chlorine bleach in each gallon water.) Dip in boiling water long enough to crack skins (about 1 minute). Dip in cold water. Peel and remove cores. Save any juice to add to the tomatoes when heating. **To pack hot:** Bring whole, peeled tomatoes to a boil. Pack immediately into hot jars. Cover with the hot liquid in which the tomatoes were heated. Add 1 teaspoon salt and 2 teaspoons vinegar or 2 teaspoons bottled lemon juice to each quart. Seal. **To pack raw:** Pack raw, whole, peeled tomatoes tightly to the tops of hot jars. Press tomatoes down after each two tomatoes are added to release juice and to fill spaces. Add 1 teaspoon salt and 2 teaspoons vinegar or 2 teaspoons bottled lemon juice to each quart. Seal. Hot pack without lemon juice or vinegar. Raw pack without lemon juice or vinegar.	15 30 30 45	15 30 30 45
TOMATO JUICE	Use sound, well-ripened, but not overripe, tomatoes. Peel, core, and cut into pieces. Either cook until soft and strain or extract juice from uncooked tomatoes. Juice from cooked tomatoes is thicker and smoother. Juice from raw tomatoes is thin and watery and tends to separate. Immediately after extracting, heat juice to simmering. Fill hot jars to ½ inch of top. Add 1 tablespoon bottled lemon juice or vinegar to each quart. Add 1 tablespoon salt to each quart or salt to taste. Seal. Process in a gently boiling water bath.	15	15

CHUNKY APPLESAUCE

My children love applesauce, and with three apple trees we have more than enough apples to fill our pantry with applesauce for the year. I used white sugar in the following recipe so the applesauce would have a lighter appearance, similar to what you buy at the market. However, when I make it for my family I use light brown sugar. My applesauce is darker and it has a rich, maplelike flavor. When adding the sugar, add ½ cup at a time until you reach the sweetness you prefer.

24 large apples

½ cup water

2 tablespoons bottled lemon juice

½ to 1½ cups sugar

3 teaspoons cinnamon

½ teaspoon nutmeg

1 teaspoon vanilla

Peel, core, and thinly slice apples. Put apples into a large saucepan with water and lemon juice. Cook covered until tender, about 20 to 25 minutes, stirring occasionally. When apples are tender, chop coarsely with a metal spoon. Add sugar, cinnamon, nutmeg, and vanilla and continue to cook until sugar dissolves. Spoon hot mixture into hot jars, to within ½ inch of top, release air bubbles, clean rims, and seal. Process in a water bath canner for 20 minutes for pints and 30 minutes for quarts.

Makes 5 pints.

APRICOTS

16 pounds apricots

6 cups sugar

8 cups water

7500 mg vitamin C tablets

Pick ripe, firm, unblemished apricots. Wash the fruit carefully, cut in half, and remove pits. Put cut fruit into water to which an anti-darkening solution of ascorbic acid has been added.

Put water and sugar into a saucepan and heat until the sugar dissolves and syrup begins to boil. Keep the liquid hot. Add one vitamin C tablet to each quart jar. Pack apricots cut side down into hot jars. Fill the jars with hot liquid to within ½ inch of the top of the jar. Remove the air bubbles and add more liquid if necessary. Wipe the rims and seal. Process in a water bath canner for 30 minutes.

Makes 7 quarts.

BRANDIED CHERRIES

You can brandy any sweet cherry. I have used the Rainier variety because of its beautiful color. It is yellow skinned and just blushed with a hint of red. Rainier cherries are large, sweet, and firm. When I can cherries I always pit them, but brandied cherries are much prettier if they are not pitted.

10 pounds Rainier cherries

2 cups sugar

2 cups water

2 tablespoons bottled lemon juice

3 tablespoons brandy per jar

Clean cherries and remove stems. Make syrup with sugar, water, and lemon juice. Cook, stirring just until syrup begins to boil. Fill clean, hot jars with cherries packed tightly. Pour hot liquid in, filling jar halfway. Add 3 tablespoons of good quality brandy, then add more hot syrup, filling the jar to within ½ inch of top. Release air bubbles and add more liquid if necessary. Clean rims, seal, and process in a water bath canner. Process pint jars for 20 minutes, 1½-pint jars for 25 minutes, and quart jars for 30 minues.

Makes 5 1½-pint jars.

© John Gajda/FPG International

MIXED FRUIT COCKTAIL

When making this fruit cocktail dice your peaches and pears into large squares. Show them off in a beautiful clear syrup that highlights the fruit's colors. A couple of helpful hints; don't pit the cherries or they will tint the syrup red. However, prick the grapes with a sterilized needle to prevent them from splitting during heating. Since the grape juice is clear it won't discolor the syrup.

3 pounds peaches (about 6 large)

3 pounds pears (about 6 large)

1 pound seedless green grapes

1 pound Royal Ann cherries

4 cups water

3 cups sugar

2 tablespoons bottled lemon juice

Peel, core, and dice the pears. Put them in an ascorbic acid solution until all the fruit is prepared. Peel, pit, and dice the peaches. Put them into the same solution as the pears. Stem and wash grapes and cherries. Heat the water, sugar, and lemon juice and cook until it just begins to boil. Drain fruit and mix all of them together. Pack fruit tightly, cut sides down, into hot jars, adding hot syrup to within ½ inch of the top of the jars. Release air bubbles, and add more liquid if necessary. Clean rims, seal, and process in a water bath canner. Process pint jars for 25 minutes and quart jars for 30 minutes.

Makes 6 pints.

LOQUATS

The loquat is a wonderful acid-sweet fruit, most often used in Chinese cooking. It is a small fruit that looks like a long apricot, and contains 3 or 4 pits. I love to just eat them off the tree, but they are wonderful when canned in a medium syrup to be enjoyed after their short season. My favorite way to use them canned is to pipe a mixture of cream cheese, orange juice concentrate, and Grand Marnier into them. This makes for a great taste treat used as an hors d'oeuvre, an accompaniment to a fruit salad, or served as a dessert along with cookies.

8 pounds loquats

3 cups sugar

4 cups water

⅓ cup bottled lemon juice

Wash and cut stem and flower ends off fruit. Cut in half and remove seeds. As you prepare fruit add it to a water-acid solution. Make your syrup, cooking the sugar, water, and lemon juice until it is ready to boil. Drain the fruit and rinse if a salt solution was used. Drop the fruit into the syrup and cook for just a couple of minutes. Pack the fruit into hot jars, cut side down, and fill to within ½ inch with hot syrup. Release air bubbles and add more liquid if necessary. Clean rims and seal. Process pint jars in a water bath canner for 15 minutes and quart jars for 20 minutes.

Makes 5 pints.

SPICED PEACHES IN PEACH WINE

These peaches are very special and make a wonderful gift.

12 pounds peaches (about 24 large)

4 cups peach wine

2 cups granulated sugar

1 cup brown sugar

¼ cup bottled lemon juice

whole stick cinnamon

whole cloves

Peel peaches and leave whole. Put the peaches in an acid solution while you peel all the fruit. Cook the wine, both sugars, lemon juice, and one whole cinnamon stick. Stir constantly until sugar dissolves and liquid begins to boil. Drain and reserve syrup. Rinse peaches if necessary. Stick one or two cloves into each peach. Add the peaches to the syrup and heat just until peaches are slightly softened. Remove pan from stove and let peaches remain in syrup overnight. This will keep them from shriveling. The next day, remove the cinnamon stick and reheat the peaches. When hot, pack the peaches as tightly as you can in hot jars. You can add one cinnamon stick per jar if you want. Cover the peaches with hot syrup, release air bubbles, and add more syrup if necessary. Clean rims and seal. Process quart jars for 20–25 minutes in a water bath canner.

Makes 6 quarts.

PEARS AND RASPBERRIES

This is a great flavor combination and makes a beautiful breakfast compote.

3 boxes raspberries (about 1½ pounds)

9 pounds pears (about 18 large)

3 tablespoons bottled lemon juice

3½ cups sugar

4 cups water

Carefully rinse and drain the raspberries. Peel, core, and dice the pears, putting diced pears in an anti-discoloration solution until all the fruit is cut. Make the syrup using lemon juice, sugar, and water. Cook the syrup until it just begins to boil. Add the pears, after they have been drained, to the syrup. Cook the pears for 3 minutes. Put pears about one-third of the way up the hot jars, then add some raspberries. Continue adding pears and raspberries until the jars are packed. Add the hot syrup and release air bubbles. Add more syrup if necessary. Clean rims, seal, and process in a water bath canner. Process quart jars for 30 minutes.

Makes 5 quarts.

CREME DE MENTHE PEARS

This is another great pear to use at Christmas time. I love to decorate my turkey platter with these pretty green pears filled with cranberry sauce.

5 pounds pears (about 10 large)

3 cups sugar

4 cups water

3 drops green food coloring

1 tablespoon fruit protector

1½ cups creme de menthe

Peel, core, and halve pears. Bring sugar, water, green food coloring, and fruit protector to a boil. Add creme de menthe and stir well. Add pears and simmer covered over low heat 3 to 5 minutes, just to heat pears through. Put the pears, cut side down, into hot jars and pack. Fill with hot cooking liquid. Release air bubbles and clean rims. Process pint jars for 20 minutes in a water bath canner.

Makes 5 pints.

CINNAMON PEARS

This will make the most beautiful Christmas gift. They are pretty to use on a Christmas fruit platter filled with a mixture of cottage cheese, nuts, and other fruits.

6 pounds pears (about 12 large)

2 cups cinnamon red hot candies

5 cups water

1 tablespoon powdered fruit protector (like Fruit Fresh™)

Peel, core, and halve pears. The core can be removed with a melon baller. Put pears into a large bowl of water with an acid solution added to prevent the fruit from darkening, until all fruit is prepared. Put the red hot candies into a large saucepan and add water. Cook and stir until candies have completely melted. Add the powdered fruit protector and stir until dissolved. Add the pears, cover, and cook 3 to 5 minutes, stirring often. Put the pears, cut side down, into hot jars and pack tightly. Fill with hot cooking liquid. Release bubbles and clean rims. Process pint jars for 20 minutes in a water bath canner.

Makes 6 pints.

STEWED PRUNES

12 cups water

4 cups sugar

¼ teaspoon salt

4 pounds prunes

1 cup plum wine

2 lemons, sliced and seeded

Bring water, sugar, and salt to a boil. Add prunes and plum wine. When prunes return to a boil add lemon slices. Cover pan and cook over low heat for 30 to 40 minutes, stirring often. Pack into hot jars and add liquid to within ½ inch of the top of the jars. Release air bubbles, clean rims, and seal. Process pint jars for 15 minutes in a water bath canner.

Makes 7 pints.

FRUIT PIE FILLINGS

Canning fruit fillings can be a little tricky. The problem is with the thickening agent you use. Fillings using cornstarch or potato starch will tend to break down in time. Flour will usually become crumbly with time. All of these thickening agents will tend to be very stiff when you use them.

The following recipes have been contributed by the USDA, which has come out with some wonderful pie fillings using a thickening agent called Clear Jel A. This is a fairly new product that is used commercially, but has not yet become well enough known to be stocked in all grocery stores. You can buy it in 400-pound sacks at $1.00 a pound or you can buy it in one pound increments for $2.49. If you wish to

order it by the pound, write to Dacus Inc., P.O. Drawer 2067, Tupelo, Mississippi, 38803.

Because these recipes using Clear Jel A are so good, I have included a few of the USDA recipes. For those unable to purchase 400 pounds of Clear Jel A, or don't want to send away for it, I have included an alternative method of making pie fillings.

I prefer to can fruit in a heavy syrup seasoned with lemon and spices. Then, when I want to make a pie, I pour the jar of fruit (a quart will make a nice 8-inch pie) in a pan and thicken it with cornstarch, then let it cool and make the pie. It is easy, not messy, and I can have fresh-tasting pies any time of the year. These fillings are also delicious cooked in breakfast pastries.

USDA APPLE PIE FILLING

	Quantities of ingredients needed for:	
	1 quart	*7 quarts*
Blanched, sliced fresh apples	3½ cups	6 quarts
Granulated sugar	¾ cup + 2 tbsp	5½ cups
Clear Jel A	¼ cup	1½ cups
Cinnamon	½ tsp	1 tbsp
Cold Water	½ cup	2½ cups
Apple juice	¾ cup	5 cups
Bottled lemon juice	2 tbsp	¾ cup
Nutmeg (optional)	⅛ tsp	1 tsp
Yellow food coloring (optional)	1 drop	7 drops

Quality: Use firm, crisp apples. Stayman, Golden Delicious, Rome, and other varieties of similar quality are suitable. If apples lack tartness, use an additional ¼ cup of lemon juice for each 6 quarts of slices. **Procedure:** Wash, peel, and core apples. Prepare slices ½ inch wide and place in water containing ascorbic acid to prevent browning. Blanch 2 quarts at a time for 1 minute in boiling water. While blanching other batches of apples, keep those already blanched in a covered pot so they will stay warm. Combine sugar, Clear Jel A, and cinnamon in a large kettle with water and apple juice. If desired, food coloring and nutmeg may be added. Stir and cook on medium-high heat until mixture thickens and begins to bubble. Drain apple slices. Add lemon juice and boil 1 minute, stirring constantly. Fold in apple slices immediately and fill jars with mixture.

BLUEBERRY PIE FILLING

4½ quarts blueberries

½ cup bottled lemon juice

rind of one lemon cut in thin strips

1 teaspoon nutmeg

1 teaspoon mace

5½ cups sugar

6½ cups water

Clean blueberries carefully and drain. Combine lemon juice, lemon rind, nutmeg, mace, sugar, and water. Cook until the mixture begins to boil. Fold in berries and cook 1 minute more. Ladle mixture into hot jars. Release air bubbles, clean rims of jars, seal, and process quart jars in a water bath canner for 30 minutes.

Makes 5 quarts.

© Steven Mark Needham/Envision

RHUBARB AND PEAR PIE FILLING

5 pounds rhubarb

4 cups sugar

4 pounds pears (about 8 large)

1 cup orange juice

1 teaspoon vanilla

6 cups water

*2 tablespoons orange peel,
    thinly sliced*

1 teaspoon mace

1 teaspoon cinnamon

Slice rhubarb in ½-inch slices. Add 2 cups of the sugar, the orange juice, and vanilla to the rhubarb in a heavy saucepan. Mix well and set aside while you prepare the pears.

Peel, core, and dice pears. Place cut pears into water containing ascorbic acid, until all pears are diced. Add the rest of the sugar, water, orange peel, mace, and cinnamon to rhubarb mixture. Stir well and bring to a boil. Drain pears and add to rhubarb mixture, cooking for 3 minutes longer. Ladle hot mixture into hot jars. Release air bubbles, clean rims of jars, and seal. Process quart jars in a water bath canner for 25 minutes.

Makes 5 quarts.

USDA CHERRY PIE FILLING

	Quantities of ingredients needed for:	
	1 quart	*7 quarts*
Fresh or thawed sour cherries	3⅓ cups	6 quarts
Granulated sugar	1 cup	7 cups
Clear Jel A	¼ cup + 1 tbsp	1¾ cups
Cold water	1⅓ cups	9⅓ cups
Bottled lemon juice	1 tbsp + 1 tsp	½ cup
Cinnamon (optional)	⅛ tsp	1 tsp
Almond extract (optional)	¼ tsp	2 tsp
Red food coloring (optional)	6 drops	¼ tsp

Quality: Select fresh, very ripe, firm cherries. Unsweetened frozen cherries may be used. If sugar has been added, rinse it off while the fruit is still frozen.

Procedure: Rinse and pit fresh cherries, and hold in cold water. To prevent stem end browning, use an ascorbic acid solution. Combine sugar and Clear Jel A in a large saucepan and add water. If desired, add cinnamon, almond extract, and food coloring. Stir mixture and cook over medium-high heat until it thickens and begins to bubble. Add lemon juice and boil 1 minute, stirring constantly. Fold in cherries immediately and fill hot jars with mixture without delay, leaving ½ inch headspace. Clean rims, adjust lids, and process in a water bath canner immediately. At altitudes of 0–1,000 feet, process pints and quarts for 30 minutes; add an additional 5 minutes to each 2,000 feet above that.

PEACH PIE FILLING

6 pounds peaches (about 12 large)

1 cup plus 2 tablespoons bottled lemon juice

3¾ cups water

5 cups sugar

2 teaspoons cinnamon

¾ teaspoon cloves

1 teaspoon nutmeg

Peel, pit, and slice peaches. To loosen skin, dip peaches in boiling water for 30 seconds, then submerge in cold water. The peaches will now peel easily. Place peach slices in water containing ascorbic acid, until all peaches are sliced. Combine lemon juice, water, sugar, cinnamon, cloves, and nutmeg in a large saucepan. Stir and cook over medium heat until mixture boils. Drain peaches and add to syrup mixture. Cook for 3 minutes. Ladle into hot jars, release air bubbles, clean jar rims, and seal. Process quart jars in a water bath canner for 30 minutes.

Makes 5 quarts.

TOMATOES

If you grow tomatoes, you know what a high-yielding fruit they are. Tomatoes are easy to preserve but must be processed at the height of flavor. They are very easy to can. All you do is peel them and pack them tightly into jars, adding salt and lemon juice. If they are packed tightly, they have plenty of their own juice for the canning liquid. Tomatoes are processed in a boiling water bath. To insure that they are acid enough and won't support the growth of botulism, add 2 tablespoons of bottled lemon juice to each quart. This not only guarantees acidity, it enhances flavor as well. I usually put up about seventy-five quarts of tomatoes a year and have great, fresh-tasting tomatoes for cooking all year long.

At this time there is some controversy over the processing time used in canning tomatoes. However, the USDA has come out with the standard safety time of processing tomatoes as being 85 minutes. It is possible that the reason for the lengthy time period for these tomatoes is because the USDA was using a very thick-skinned (like Italian tomatoes) unpeeled tomato. This particular type of thick-skinned tomato, with the skin left on, would take 85 minutes to penetrate the heat needed to safely process.

CANNED TOMATOES

These are the tomatoes I use in cooking sauces and soups all year. Because they are canned at the peak of their flavor, they are far superior to the tomatoes available most of the year.

35 to 40 large tomatoes

1 teaspoon sugar per quart (optional)

1 teaspoon salt per quart (optional)

2 tablespoons bottled lemon juice

Peel the tomatoes by dropping them into boiling water for 15 seconds. Core each tomato and leave it whole. Put salt, sugar, and lemon juice into hot jars. Pack tomatoes tightly into the jars. You should have plenty of juice to cover the tomatoes by pressing them down. Remove air bubbles and clean the rim of the jars. Seal and process in a water bath canner. Process quart jars for 45 minutes.

Makes 7 quarts.

FRESH BASIL TOMATO SAUCE

This is one of my family's favorites. It is light and low in calories, but full of spicy flavor.

3 tablespoons olive oil

3 onions, minced

3 garlic cloves, minced

2 tablespoons fresh basil, chopped or 1 tablespoon dried basil

3 tablespoons minced parsley

25 to 30 tomatoes

2 teaspoons salt

2 teaspoons pepper

1½ teaspoons sugar

1 tablespoon plus 1 teaspoon beef bouillon

Add oil to a 6-quart pot. Mince onions and garlic in food processor and sauté in oil until transparent. Add basil and parsley. Peel tomatoes (dip in boiling water 15 seconds and peel) and process until like juice. Add to pot with onions and herbs. Add the rest of the ingredients and blend well. Cook on low heat for 1½ hours, stirring often. When sauce is done, ladle into hot jars to within ½ inch of the top of the jar. Clean rims and seal. Process for 45 minutes in a water bath canner.

Makes 6 quarts.

PIZZA SAUCE

This sauce is great on home-made pizza, but don't stop there. Spoon some sauce over sautéed chicken and melt mozzarella on it. It's wonderful!

25 to 28 tomatoes

2 large onions, minced

4 garlic cloves, minced

3 tablespoons olive oil

2 tablespoons lemon juice

1 teaspoon cracked pepper

1 tablespoon sugar

2 tablespoons parsley, chopped

1 tablespoon oregano

1 tablespoon basil

1 teaspoon rosemary

1 teaspoon celery seed

2 teaspoons salt

½ teaspoon summer savory

Peel and puree tomatoes. Mince onions and garlic. Put olive oil in a large, deep pan and sauté onions and garlic until transparent. Add tomato puree and the rest of the ingredients. Stir well to blend and continue cooking over low heat until mixture is reduced by half. Stir occasionally. This will take 1½ to 2 hours to reduce. When sauce is done and nicely thickened, ladle into hot pint size jars. Clean rims of jars, and seal. Process pint jars for 25 minutes in a water bath canner.

Makes 4–5 pints.

TOMATO SAUCE

21 pounds tomatoes (about 63)

2 onions

1 large green bell pepper

2 stalks celery

½ cup bottled lemon juice

1 tablespoon sugar

1 tablespoon salt

1½ teaspoons black pepper

⅓ cup chopped parsley

Peel tomatoes and puree in a tomato press or in batches in a food processor. Put into a large pan. Process onions, bell pepper, and celery together and mince finely. Add to tomatoes. Add the rest of the ingredients and mix well. Cook over medium heat, stirring occasionally, until mixture thickens and has reduced by almost half. Ladle hot mixture into hot jars. Clean rims of jars, seal, and process in a water bath canner for 35 minutes.

Makes 7 pints.

FANCY KETCHUP

This ketchup has a wonderful taste; the apple lends a nice sweetness. I used a great tomato press I bought from Williams-Sonoma. Put the tomatoes in the press, crank it, and the seeds and skins come out one spout, while the puree comes out another. The Cuisinart strainer attachment also works well for this purpose.

25 to 30 tomatoes

4 apples

1 onion

1 cup cider vinegar

3 tablespoons brown sugar

1 teaspoon oregano

½ teaspoon chili powder

3 whole bay leaves

Peel and core tomatoes. Puree in a processor or push the tomatoes through a strainer into a large 6- to 8-quart enamel or stainless steel pan. Peel, core, and slice apples. Put them in a pan with 1 cup of water. Cover and cook for 15 to 20 minutes until soft. Process (or use the tomato press) the apples to a fine puree. Add to the tomatoes. Add all the rest of the ingredients and cook on low heat stirring often, for 2 hours or until proper consistency of ketchup is reached. Ladle hot ketchup into hot jars. Clean rims of jars, seal, and process in a water bath canner for 45 minutes for ½-pint jars or pint jars.

Makes 4 half-pints.

SALSA

5½ pounds tomatoes, peeled and diced (about 16 to 17 medium size)

2 onions, diced

1 can (7 ounces) chilis, diced

2 teaspoons salt

1 teaspoon cracked pepper

2 tablespoons bottled lemon juice

2 tablespoons chopped cilantro

½ cup vinegar

1½ teaspoons cayenne pepper

Combine all ingredients and mix well. Heat salsa just until hot. Ladle into hot jars. Clean rims, seal, and process in a water bath canner for 45 minutes.

Makes 6 pints.

CHAPTER THREE

JAMS, JELLIES, AND PRESERVES

In the summer, my favorite time of day is the early morning, when the sun is shining and casting shadows across my kitchen. The French doors are open and sweet smells sweep through the house, while on my stove is a copper jelly pan full of softly boiling, beautifully colored fruit.

There is nothing nicer than starting your day with a wonderful homemade jam spread on a fresh baked biscuit. When you start preserving you will be excited with all the fruit combinations you can create. Once you have started feeding your family and friends these homemade preserves it will be hard to go back to store bought.

Many different kinds of preserves can be made with fruit. They change by adding ingredients to the fruit, or as with jelly, extracting the juice from the fruit. You can have lots of fun with your imagination and can easily create your own recipes.

The many types of preserves are defined below.

FRUIT BUTTERS: Butters are made from purees of fruit to which sugar and spices have been added. Butters are cooked very slowly on the stove, in the oven, or in a crock pot, stirring often so that it won't burn. The mixture is cooked until it is very thick and spreadable.

CONSERVES: Combinations of two or more fruits, cooked to a jamlike consistency, usually adding nuts or raisins to the mixture.

JAMS: Crushed or chopped fruit cooked to a smooth, thick consistency that is easily spread.

JELLIES: Clear and beautifully colored, jellies are made from the juice of the fruit. It is not as thick as jam and should quiver (shake like partially set jello) when spooned.

MARMALADES: Like bright jellies with suspended fruit and slivers of citrus.

PRESERVES: Brightly colored, having tender chunks of the fruit or a combination of fruits. If the consistency is correct, the fruit pieces are beautifully suspended in the jar.

Following are recipes for all these different categories of preserves, as well as a few jam and jelly recipes that have little or no sugar. These no-sugar recipes have been devised at the University of California at Davis, by the Division of Agricultural Sciences.

METHODS FOR MAKING JAMS, PRESERVES, MARMALADES, AND CONSERVES

Prepare your jars and lids; wash and sterilize jars and rings.

Prepare your fruit by washing, peeling, pitting, cutting, or leaving whole.

Decide if you will use pectin or the long boil method. If you use pectin, follow my directions for the short boil method or follow the directions that come with the pectin. If you use the long boil method cook until the jell point is reached. (Measure the temperature of water at a full boil and add 8°F more for the jell point. It is 220°F at sea level.)

Remove from heat and wait 5 minutes, skimming off any foam that forms. This 5-minute wait also helps the fruit to cool just enough so it will suspend nicely in the jar and not all rise to the top.

Fill hot, sterilized jars with your preserves. Wipe the rims and seal the jars.

Process the jars in a boiling water bath for 10 minutes. This will insure a good seal.

Check your seal by pressing down on the lid about 2 hours after processing. The lid should not move. If it does, open it, clean the rims, reseal with a new lid, and reprocess. You can also refrigerate and use the jam if it didn't seal. But if you follow directions, you should have a great seal.

You can also seal with paraffin, melting it in a metal cup in a pan of water. Pour about ⅛ inch in the jar and turn the jar so the paraffin touches all sides for a good seal. Wait a couple of minutes and add ⅛ inch more.

Store your preserves in a cool, dry, dark place. If juices and fruit preserves are stored in a sunlit area the color may darken over time.

JELLIES

Jellies are clear and beautifully colored. They are made from the juice of fruit. You can use commercially bought juices (like grape, apple, or cranberry) to make jellies or you can prepare and cook your fruit then strain out the juice. You can also use frozen fruit. Mash it and add sugar to draw the juice out. Let it set for an hour or so before straining it.

Begin by picking out your fruit. Then peel, pit, and slice it, or chop it in a food processor. You are trying to get as much juice from the fruit as possible. It is best not to dilute your fruit juice, but when you are cooking apples or plums they tend to burn if some water is not added when cooking. Add ¼ cup of water per pound of fruit when cooking. Cook the fruit until it is soft, 10 to 20 minutes. Then pour the mixture into a suspended jelly bag and let the juice drip. You could also use cheesecloth or muslin folded in a strainer or colander and let it drip into a bowl. Never squeeze the jelly bag or cheesecloth to get more juice. You will have cloudy jelly. Plan to have enough time to let it drip. You can always refrigerate or freeze the juice to make jelly at another time.

With berries you can add some sugar and mash them. Letting them sit for an hour or so before straining will help to draw the juice out.

Once you have the juice you can use the short boil method or the long boil method.

The **Short Boil** method is when you use pectin as your jelling agent. Bring the fruit or juice to a boil, add lemon juice if called for, and pectin. Bring the fruit to a rolling boil again. Never add sugar first if you use pectin. You must add the pectin first, before the sugar, or it will not jell. Add the required amount of sugar and bring back to a boil that cannot be stirred down. Boil 1 minute more. Remove from heat and skim any foam that has formed. Pour into hot jars and seal. It is always a good idea to read all directions that come with your pectin.

The **Long Boil** method is when no pectin is used. If you are unsure of the pectin level of the fruit, add some lemon

juice. This method allows you to use less sugar than the short boil method. Combine all your ingredients and boil until your jell point is reached (8°F above the point at which water will boil.) The jell point is 220°F at sea level.

PROBLEMS YOU MAY HAVE WITH JAMS AND JELLIES	
Jam or jelly too hard.	Cooked too long and/or too much pectin added.
Jam or jelly too soft.	You did not cook long enough or you did not follow the recipe and use the right amount of sugar or pectin. Also never try to make too much at once. Make only one recipe at a time.
Cloudy jelly.	You may have squeezed your jelly bag to extract juice.
Fruit at top of jars.	Be sure to cool the jam or preserves 5 minutes before putting in the jar. This will let the fruit suspend nicely in the jar.
Darkening of jam or jelly.	You may have stored your preserves in too light of a place. They need to be stored in a dark, dry, cool place.
Weeping (liquid on the top) jam.	Too much acid in the juice or too thick a layer of paraffin.
Sugar crystals.	You may have used too much sugar or you may have cooked the jelly too long. Try to follow the recipes as close as possible.

MINT APPLE JELLY

4 cups apple juice

1 cup mint leaves

1 package (2 ounces) powdered fruit pectin

3½ tablespoons bottled lemon juice

3½ cups sugar

3 or 4 drops green food coloring

Bring apple juice to a boil. Chop mint leaves in a food processor and add to apple juice. Boil 1 minute. Remove saucepan from heat and let stand covered for 15 to 20 minutes. Return to heat and bring to a boil again. Boil 30 seconds more. Pour apple juice and mint into a jelly bag and strain the juice. Do not squeeze the jelly bag. Return the apple juice to the pan and stir in the lemon juice and pectin. Bring to a boil again, stirring constantly. Add sugar all at once and stir well to dissolve. Bring back to a rolling boil and boil hard for 1 minute, stirring constantly. Remove from heat and add food coloring. Skim off any foam and ladle into hot jars leaving ¼-inch headspace. Clean rims, seal, and process in a hot water bath for 10 minutes.

Makes 5 half-pint jars.

CURRANT JELLY

3 pounds red currants

2 cups water

3⅓ cups sugar

Wash currants in a strainer. When clean, put currants and 2 cups of water into a heavy saucepan. Boil for 5 minutes. Stir to slightly crush berries. Remove from heat and pour into a jelly bag to strain. You should get about 4 cups of juice. Put juice in a heavy pan and add sugar. Cook, stirring often, and skim foam as it accumulates. When the jell point is reached, remove from heat and skim the foam again. Ladle into hot jars. Clean rims and seal. Process in a water bath canner for 10 minutes.

Makes 4 half-pint jars.

POMEGRANATE JELLY

This jelly is a beautiful clear color. It makes a wonderful Christmas present. Before I owned a food processor this jelly took forever to make; trying to extract the juice from those little seeds drove me crazy. Now that I have the Cuisinart strainer attachment it is really easy. A little hint: If you use the strainer attachment, cover the top with a paper towel so you don't get any juice stains on you.

10 pomegranates

⅓ cup bottled lemon juice

1 package (2 ounces) powdered fruit pectin

5 cups sugar

© Maggie Oster

To extract the juice from pomegranates, first score each piece of fruit about five times and pull apart under water. You do this because the juice will stain clothing. After you have removed the seeds, swirl them in a food processor, using the metal blade, until the fruit is juicy. Put into a jelly bag and let it strain overnight. Put the juice (you'll have about 4 cups), lemon juice, and pectin into a pan. Stir and bring to a rolling boil. Stirring constantly, add the sugar all at once and continue to stir while the jelly boils hard for 1 minute. Remove from heat and skim any foam that has formed. Ladle the hot mixture into hot jars, clean rims, and seal. Process in a water bath canner for 10 minutes.

Makes 5 half-pint jars.

WHITE ZINFANDEL JELLY

This is a very pretty jelly. It could be made with any wine, but I love the color of the jelly when you use a deep-colored zinfandel.

2 cups white zinfandel wine

3 cups sugar

1 pouch liquid pectin

Mix the wine and sugar in the top of a double boiler. Heat, stirring until all the sugar melts; this will take 4 to 5 minutes. Remove from heat and stir in liquid pectin. Pour into hot jars to within ⅛ inch of the top. Clean rims and seal with a thin layer of paraffin.

Makes 4 or 5 half-pint jars.

PEPPER JELLY

A very good friend of mine, Samone August, gave me this recipe for a pepper jelly. It is really different and tastes great. She got it from a friend of hers years ago, and it is well worth passing on. Try serving it on top of crackers that have been spread with cream cheese, or on a grilled turkey or chicken sandwich. It's a great treat with champagne or any before-dinner drink.

*2 medium-size green
    bell peppers*

*½ cup fresh hot chili peppers
    or ½ cup canned chilis*

1½ cups cider vinegar

6 cups sugar

*6 ounces (2 envelopes)
    liquid pectin*

Remove stems and seeds from peppers. Grind peppers in a food processor until liquified. Measure ¾ cup into a heavy saucepan. Grind the hot chilis in the same way and add to the pan with the peppers. Add the vinegar and sugar. Bring to a full rolling boil, stirring constantly. Add pectin and stir until well blended. Bring back to a full rolling boil and boil for 1 minute. Remove from heat and skim foam with a metal spoon. Ladle into hot jars and seal. Process in a water bath canner for 5 minutes.

Makes 7 half-pint jars.

JAMS

Jams are made from crushed fruits. Once you have mastered making jams you will love making preserves, marmalades, and conserves. These all really only add ingredients, but use the same cooking process as jams.

Jams are made by using the short boil or long boil method described in the jelly section (see page 54). However, jams can also be made with the no-cook method.

The no-cook method, which is often called freezer jam, uses pectin. Prepare your fruit. Crush it or spin it in your food processor. Add the sugar and lemon juice and let it stand for 20 to 30 minutes to draw the juices out. Then put your box of pectin in 1 cup of cold water and stir to dissolve. Bring to a boil and boil for 1 minute. Stir into the fruit mixture that has been standing at room temperature; stir thoroughly for another 2 minutes. Pour into sterilized jars and seal. Check for consistency after a few hours. If it has jelled nicely you can put it in the freezer. If it has not yet jelled, leave in the refrigerator for 2 to 3 days before freezing. This will let it set. Jam prepared this way can be stored in the refrigerator 2 to 3 weeks or in the freezer for a year.

The no-cook method uses the most sugar, 2 cups to one cup of fruit. The jam will be very fresh tasting and sugar does enhance the flavor of jams. So, even though this method requires quite a lot of sugar, there are only about 50 to 60 calories a tablespoon. The long boil method uses the least sugar, cooking the mixture until the desired thickness is reached. With the short boil method you must use the required amount of sugar—usually 1½ cups sugar to 1 cup of fruit—along with the pectin or it will not jell properly.

© Priscilla Connell/Photo/Nats

PEACH JAM

*4 pounds peaches (about
    8 large)*

*2 tablespoons bottled
    lemon juice*

5 cups sugar

½ teaspoon nutmeg

Prepare peaches by peeling, pitting, and cutting into quarters. Chop in a food processor or cut into small pieces. Put peaches, lemon juice, sugar, and nutmeg in a saucepan and cook over medium heat, stirring to dissolve all the sugar. Boil rapidly and stir constantly until the jam is thick or has reached the jell point on a thermometer. Remove from heat and let stand 5 minutes, skimming off any foam. Ladle into hot jars, clean rims, seal, and process in a water bath canner for 10 minutes.

Makes 5 half-pint jars.

PEACH-RASPBERRY
JAM

3 large peaches

1 cup raspberries

¼ cup bottled lemon juice

6 cups sugar

*1 package (2 ounces)
    powdered fruit pectin*

Peel, pit, and slice peaches. Whirl peaches in the food processor until coarsely chopped. Clean raspberries carefully. Put peaches, raspberries, lemon juice, and pectin into a large saucepan. Bring to a boil, stirring constantly. Add sugar all at once and stir until mixture comes to a rolling boil. Boil rapidly for 1 minute. Let jam sit for 5 minutes while you skim off any foam. Ladle into hot jars, clean rims, seal, and process in a water bath canner for 10 minutes.

Makes 7 half-pints.

© Bruce Byers/FPG International

RHUBARB-PEACH JAM

1½ pounds rhubarb

½ cup water

¼ cup bottled lemon juice

1 pound peaches (about 2 large)

4½ cups sugar

1½ tablespoons crystallized ginger, finely diced

Wash and cut rhubarb into ½-inch pieces. Put rhubarb, water, and lemon juice into a saucepan and bring to a boil. Remove from heat, stir well, and let stand for 1 hour. Peel, pit, and dice peaches. Add peaches, sugar, and ginger to rhubarb mixture. Bring mixture to a boil, stirring constantly. Cook over medium heat until jam is thick and clear, or reaches the jell point on a thermometer. Skim foam as jam cooks. Remove from heat and let sit 5 minutes. Skim off any more foam that rises. Ladle into hot, sterilized jars, clean rims, seal, and process in a water bath canner for 5 minutes.

Makes 6 half-pints.

APRICOT-PINEAPPLE JAM

Heat this jam with soy sauce and white wine and baste a pork tenderloin with the mixture in the oven or on a grill.

7 pounds apricots

2 cans (8¾ ounces each) crushed pineapple in heavy syrup (do not drain)

⅓ cup bottled lemon juice

6 cups sugar

1 teaspoon cinnamon

¾ teaspoon nutmeg

Wash and pit apricots. Dice in a food processor. Put apricots, undrained pineapple, lemon juice, sugar, cinnamon, and nutmeg into a large saucepan. Over low heat, stir until sugar melts. Bring to a boil and boil softly, stirring often, until jam is thick and clear, or registers 220°F on the thermometer. Skim off foam while cooking. Remove from heat and let sit 5 minutes. Skim off any foam. Ladle into hot, sterilized jars, clean rims, seal, and process in a water bath canner for 5 minutes.

Makes 5 pints.

CHERRY-BLUEBERRY JAM

3 cups cherries, pitted

3 cups blueberries

1 tablespoon lemon rind, thinly sliced

2 tablespoons bottled lemon juice

4½ cups sugar

½ teaspoon nutmeg

Clean and pit cherries. Clean blueberries. Put cherries, blueberries, lemon rind, and lemon juice, sugar, and nutmeg into a large saucepan. Cook the mixture, stirring constantly until sugar melts. Boil mixture softly until it thickens or reaches the jell point. Ladle into hot jars, clean rims, seal, and process for 10 minutes in a water bath canner.

Makes 5 half-pint jars.

COOKING JAMS AND JELLIES WITH LITTLE OR NO SUGAR

In today's diet-conscious society, less sugar is very important. Also, many medical diets call for less sugar. I have included a few recipes devised by the University of California at Davis, using much less sugar than most jams and jellies. The University of Davis suggests removing excess liquid from the fruit before making the jam. By doing this and cooking the pulp you will have a much thicker jam, naturally.

To remove the excess liquid:

1. Wash and prepare your fruit. Remove pits, stems, or seeds, and peel if necessary.
2. Cut or chop your fruit in a processor or mash with a fork.
3. Cook the fruit in a pan for a few minutes to release the juices.
4. Pour the fruit into a jelly bag and let the juice drain for 15 minutes.
5. Save the juice for jelly or fruit juice.
6. Measure the solid fruit and use for making jams with little or no sugar.

When using less sugar or no sugar, you can freeze the jam or process it. Processed jam with little or no sugar may change color slightly over time; if it is frozen, however, it will retain its color better. If gelatin is used as a thickening agent in the jam or jelly it must not be processed. All jams and jellies should be refrigerated and used within a month.

If you wish to use artificial sweeteners they need to be added after cooking the jam or jelly or it will have a bitter taste. Some people prefer to wait until the jam is opened and then stir in the artificial sweetener.

LOW-SUGAR PEACH-PINEAPPLE JAM

This first recipe is from the University of California at Davis, and they have given the calorie count for the different levels of sugar used.

You can determine what calorie intake is best for you and what tastes best. You can then figure out the other recipes accordingly.

	Little sugar 1 level tbsp. 22 calories (per level tbsp.)	Less sugar 1 level tbsp. 15 calories (per level tbsp.)	No sugar 1 level tbsp. 8 calories (per level tbsp.)
Drained peach pulp	4 cups	4 cups	4 cups
Drained unsweetened crushed pineapple	2 cups	2 cups	2 cups
Bottled lemon juice	¼ cup	¼ cup	¼ cup
Sugar	2 cups	1 cup	0*

Place drained cooked peaches, drained crushed pineapple, lemon juice, and sugar in a 4-quart saucepan. Mix well to dissolve sugar. Bring to a boil, stirring constantly. Boil to the desired thickness, 10 to 15 minutes, stirring occasionally to prevent scorching.

To freeze jam: Remove from heat. Add calorie-free sweetener if desired. Continue to stir about 2 minutes. Pour into freezer containers, leaving ½-inch headspace. Seal. Chill in refrigerator, then store in freezer. Keep in refrigerator after opening.

Whereas low-sugar jams will retain color better if stored in a freezer, it is safe to can them by the boiling water bath method.

To can jam: Pour boiling hot jam into clean, hot pint or half-pint canning jars to ¼-inch from top of jar. Seal and process in boiling water bath, 15 minutes for half-pint jars, 20 minutes for pint jars. Cool and store in cool, dry, dark place. After opening, store in refrigerator.

*You may wish to add a powdered calorie-free sweetener. Equivalents will be stated on the box.

Makes 4 or 5 half-pint jars, depending on how much sugar is used.

LOW-SUGAR PLUM-PEACH JAM WITH PECTIN

3 cups firm, ripe Santa Rosa plums (about 1½ pounds), chopped

2 cups firm, ripe peaches, peeled and sliced (about 4 large)

1 package (1¾ or 2 ounce) powdered fruit pectin

1 cup sugar (for a more tart jam use only ½ cup sugar)

Grind fruit with medium blade of food processor. If any juice is released drain before making jam. Stir ground fruit, pectin, and sugar in saucepan to dissolve sugar. Bring to a boil and boil 10 to 15 minutes until thickened. Stir constantly.

To freeze: Remove from heat. Pour into clean, hot freezer jars, leaving ½-inch headspace. Cover, chill, and freeze. Thaw before using. Store in refrigerator after opening.

To can: Pour boiling hot jam into clean, hot canning jars to ¼ inch from top of jar. Seal and process in a boiling water bath. Process half-pint jars for 15 minutes. Process pint jars for 20 minutes. Cool and store in a cool, dark, dry place. After opening, store in the refrigerator.

1 tablespoon = 15 calories.

Makes 4 half-pint jars.

SPICED NO-SUGAR APPLE JELLY

2 envelopes unflavored gelatin

4 cups apple juice

2 whole sticks cinnamon

4 whole cloves

2 tablespoons bottled lemon juice

2 drops yellow food coloring

From 1 teaspoon to 1 tablespoon liquid calorie-free sweetener (depending on sweetness desired)

Soften gelatin in apple juice in medium-sized saucepan. Add cinnamon sticks, cloves, and lemon juice. Bring slowly to rolling boil, stirring to dissolve gelatin. Boil 2 minutes. Remove from heat. Remove spices. Stir in calorie-free sweetener and food coloring. Pour into hot jelly jars. Seal. Chill and store in refrigerator. This jelly will keep well in refrigerator from 4 to 6 weeks. Do not freeze.

1 tablespoon = 9 calories

Makes 3 half-pint jars.

NO-SUGAR PEACH JAM WITH PECTIN

4 cups peeled, sliced, firm, ripe peaches (about 3 large)

1 package (1¾ or 2 ounces) powdered fruit pectin

1 tablespoon bottled lemon juice

½ teaspoon liquid calorie-free sweetener (more or less according to taste)

½ teaspoon ascorbic acid

Grind peaches in a food grinder with medium or coarse blade or crush peaches with fork. If peaches are juicy, drain to remove some liquid before making jam. In a saucepan, stir fruit pectin, lemon juice, and ascorbic acid into ground peaches. Bring to a boil and boil 1 minute, stirring constantly. Remove from heat, add calorie-free sweetener, and stir thoroughly.

To freeze jam: Continue to stir for 2 minutes. Pour into clean, hot freezer jars leaving ½-inch headspace. Seal, chill, and freeze. Thaw before serving. Store in refrigerator after opening.

To can jam: Pour hot jam into clean, hot, canning jars to ¼ inch from the top. Seal and process in boiling water bath. Process pint jars for 20 minutes, half-pint jars for 15 minutes. Cool and store in a cool, dark, dry place. After opening, store in the refrigerator.

1 tablespoon = 8 calories

Makes 2 half-pint jars.

NO-SUGAR GRAPE JELLY

1 envelope unflavored gelatin

2 cups unsweetened grape juice (any other unsweetened juice can be used)

1 tablespoon bottled lemon juice

1¾ teaspoons liquid calorie-free sweetener (use more or less according to taste)

Add gelatin to grape juice and lemon juice in a saucepan. Place over low heat. Stir constantly until gelatin dissolves. Bring to a boil and boil 1½ to 2 minutes. Remove from heat. Add calorie-free sweetener. Stir well to mix. Pour into clean hot jars. Seal. Cool and store in refrigerator. This jelly will keep well in a refrigerator 4 to 6 weeks. Do not freeze.

1 tablespoon = 10 calories

Makes 2 half-pint jars.

NO-COOK (FREEZER) JAM

I have a very good friend, Jill Presson, who taught me how to make freezer jam. When I first tasted the jam I could not believe how fresh tasting it was. It was like eating just-picked fruit. Also, its color is just beautiful. The peach is bright yellow and the strawberry is the prettiest light red. You will find this very easy to make, and if you use a food processor to chop the fruit, you will have very little mess. These jams are great any way, but my family loves them on pancakes.

STRAWBERRY NO-COOK JAM

Mix a jar of this jam with a large container of Cool Whip® and one small carton of strawberry yogurt for a beautiful fruit dip.

2 cups crushed strawberries

4 cups sugar

2 tablespoons bottled lemon juice

1 package (2 ounces) powdered fruit pectin

1 cup cold water

Clean strawberries and whirl in a food processor until crushed. Add sugar and lemon juice and let the fruit stand for 20 to 30 minutes to draw out the juices. Put pectin into 1 cup cold water in saucepan and stir to dissolve. Bring to a rolling boil and boil for 1 minute. Pour pectin mixture into fruit and stir thoroughly for 2 minutes. Ladle into hot jars leaving ½-inch headspace, wipe rims, and seal. Store in freezer or refrigerator after the jam has cooled.

Makes 7 half-pints.

PEACH NO-COOK JAM

You can use many other fruits when making no-cook jams. Follow the general recipe given here, making sure you only use 2 cups of fruit. Always make only one batch at a time or you will not get a good jell. Other good fruits for this jam are cherries, plums, apricots, and raspberries.

2 pounds peaches (about 4 large)

4 cups sugar

3 tablespoons lemon juice

1 package (2 ounces) powdered fruit pectin

Peel, pit, and crush peaches. Add sugar and lemon juice. Let mixture stand at room temperature for 20 to 30 minutes to draw out juices. Put pectin into 1 cup cold water in a saucepan and stir until well mixed. Bring pectin to a rolling boil and boil for 1 minute. Stir pectin into fruit mixture constantly for 2 minutes. Ladle into hot jars, wipe rims, and seal. Let cool and store in the refrigerator for 2 to 3 weeks, or in the freezer for up to a year.

Makes 4 to 5 half-pints.

PRESERVES

Preserves, marmalades, and conserves are basically made like jams; however, you add other ingredients. Preserves are closest to jams except that they use large pieces or even whole pieces of fruit instead of mashed or crushed fruit like jam. Marmalades are like a nice jelly but have slivers of citrus peel in them. Conserves, like jam, can use a combination of more than one fruit. Conserves also contain nuts, raisins, or dried fruit.

Preserves, marmalades, or conserves can be cooked the short boil or long boil method just like jam. The equipment needed and procedures for cooking are the same as for jams.

PROPER EQUIPMENT FOR FRUIT PRESERVES

A **deep, flat-bottomed pan** large enough so the mixture can boil without boiling over the pan. Enamel, stainless steel, or an unlined copper jelly pan are best to use.

A **jelly thermometer** is helpful in checking for the jelling point, which is 8°F higher than the point of boiling water.

A **food processor** or **food mill** helps so much when you chop or grind the fruit. Also, the Cuisinart strainer attachment makes butters and jellies a snap.

A **jelly bag** for extracting the juice from fruits. You can also use cheesecloth or muslin in a suspended strainer.

A **timer** is very important especially if you are using pectin as a thickener.

Funnels will really help to keep your jars clean and make less mess.

Measuring spoons and **cups** are a necessity for proper measuring of ingredients.

A **scale** is helpful in measuring the amount of fruit, and it will help you to determine the correct amount of sugar needed.

Jars and **lids**.

Metal cup or **small pan** if you use paraffin.

A **boiling water canner** or **large kettle** for processing.

A **jar lifter**.

© Bruce Byers/FPG International

PEACH PRESERVES

This preserve gives you a wonderful summer taste all year.

3½ pounds peaches (about 7)

¼ cup bottled lemon juice

5 cups sugar

¾ teaspoon almond extract

Peel, pit, and coarsely dice peaches. Cut peaches into water that has ascorbic acid added until all peaches are cut. Rinse peaches and put them into a heavy saucepan. Add lemon juice and sugar. Heat to boiling, stirring constantly, until sugar is dissolved. Reduce heat so you have a slow boil and cook until fruit is translucent and thick, stirring occasionally. Stir in almond extract. Remove from heat and skim off any foam that rises. Ladle into hot jars, clean rims, seal, and process for 10 minutes in a water bath canner.

Makes 6 to 7 pints.

STRAWBERRY-PEACH PRESERVES

4 baskets strawberries (2 quarts)

2 pounds peaches (4 large)

3 tablespoons bottled lemon juice

5½ cups sugar

Clean strawberries. Cut large ones into quarters and small ones in half. Peel and pit peaches and cut into small pieces. Put fruit, lemon juice, and sugar into a large heavy saucepan. Stir over medium heat until all sugar is dissolved. Bring to a boil and cook at a slow boil, stirring often until the preserves are thick and have a transparent look. Ladle into hot jars, clean rims, and seal. Process in a water bath canner for 10 minutes.

Makes 7 half-pints.

PEACH-PINEAPPLE PRESERVES

I remember my Mom and Dad making this recipe every year. We all loved it and it was great on our Thanksgiving ham. Try it on a pork loin roast done on the barbecue. You'll love it.

5 pounds peaches (about 10 large)

2 cans (8¾ ounces each) crushed pineapple (do not drain)

⅓ cup bottled lemon juice

5 cups sugar

1 teaspoon cinnamon

½ teaspoon nutmeg

¼ teaspoon mace

Peel, pit, and large dice peaches. Put cut peaches into water containing ascorbic acid so that peaches don't change color, until all peaches are cut. Rinse peaches and put into a heavy saucepan. Add undrained pineapple, lemon juice, sugar, cinnamon, nutmeg, and mace. Bring to a boil, dissolving the sugar. Turn heat down and cook at a slow boil until preserves are thick and translucent. Remove from heat, remove any foam with a metal spoon, ladle into hot jars, clean rims, and seal. Process in water bath canner for 10 minutes.

Makes 5 to 6 pints.

© John Mutrux

© Hanson Carroll

APPLE-PEAR PRESERVES

2½ pounds pears (about 5 large)

2½ pounds apples (about 5 large)

¼ cup bottled lemon juice

6 cups sugar

1 teaspoon cinnamon

¼ teaspoon ground allspice

2 teaspoons ground ginger

Peel, core, and coarsely chop pears. Put cut pears into water containing ascorbic acid, until all fruit is prepared. Peel, core, and coarsely chop apples. Add to pears in water until all fruit is diced. Rinse fruit and put in a heavy saucepan. Add lemon juice, sugar, cinnamon, allspice, and ginger to fruit. Stir well, heating to dissolve sugar. Bring mixture to a boil, reduce heat, and cook at a slow boil. Remove foam as it forms. Cook, stirring and skimming until preserves have thickened and become translucent. Mash fruit slightly with a potato masher. Remove from heat and let sit 5 minutes. While it rests skim off any foam that has formed. Ladle into hot jars, clean rims, seal, and process 10 minutes in a water bath canner.

Makes 4 half-pints.

STRAWBERRY PRESERVES

I just love strawberry preserves because they are so versatile. They are delicious when used in a trifle, baked in the middle of a breakfast pastry, or dabbed in the center of your favorite sugar cookie.

8 cups strawberries

*2 tablespoons bottled
    lemon juice*

5 cups sugar

Clean and stem strawberries. Cut strawberries in half. Put berries, lemon juice, and sugar into a large heavy saucepan. Stir, bringing the mixture to a boil. Cook the mixture on medium heat until the preserves thicken and become transparent. Remove pan from heat. Skim off foam that has formed, and ladle into hot jars. Seal and process in a water bath canner for 10 minutes.

Makes 7 half-pint jars.

CHERRY PRESERVES

Put a teaspoon of these preserves into your Christmas thumbprint cookies.

*6 cups sweet cherries
    (3 pounds)*

4 cups sugar

*3 tablespoons bottled
    lemon juice*

½ teaspoon almond extract

Wash and pit cherries, or cut in half and remove pits. Put cherries, sugar, and lemon juice in a heavy saucepan. Mix well and warm on stove 5 minutes, stirring constantly. Remove from heat and let stand 1 hour. This is to draw the juice out. Return to heat, add almond extract, and cook, stirring occasionally until thick and glossy. Continue cooking until the jell point is reached (220°F at sea level). Skim foam as necessary. Remove from heat, ladle into hot jars, clean rims, seal, and process for 10 minutes in a water bath canner.

Makes 5 to 6 half-pints.

© Maggie Oster

GOOSEBERRY PRESERVES

Gooseberries take a while to prepare. Removing the stem and tail on each berry is time-consuming, but the preserve is a very pretty color and you will be pleased with your efforts.

4 cups gooseberries

3 cups sugar

*3 tablespoons bottled
    lemon juice*

Wash berries carefully and remove stems and tails. Put into a heavy saucepan with the sugar and lemon juice. Cook over medium heat until all sugar is dissolved, stirring constantly. Cook at a slow boil until the preserves are thick and slightly transparent. Remove from heat before ladling into hot jars. Clean rims, seal, and process in a water bath canner for 10 minutes.

Makes 4 half-pints.

MARMALADES

Marmalades are so pretty. They look like a beautiful jelly with floating slices of citrus peel or small fruits. To make the peels and fruits float throughout the marmalade (and not rise to the top), make sure to let the marmalade cool slightly before ladling into jars.

PINK GRAPEFRUIT MARMALADE

3 pink grapefruit

4 cups unsweetened grapefruit juice

¼ cup bottled lemon juice

1 package (2 ounces) powdered fruit pectin

6½ cups sugar

1 teaspoon vanilla

Peel grapefruit and put peel in a saucepan with 1 cup of water. Boil 5 minutes, drain, and put in a pan with 1 more cup of water; boil 5 more minutes. Drain and repeat one more time. Slice peel into thin slivers. Put peel into a pan with a cup of water again and boil; this time cover and leave overnight. The next day, put the drained peel in a heavy saucepan, add the unsweetened grapefruit juice, lemon juice, and pectin. Stir and bring to a rolling boil. Make sure the pectin has dissolved. With the juice at a rolling boil, add the sugar all at once. Bring the mixture back to a boil that can not be stirred down. Boil hard for 4 minutes. Remove foam as it cooks. After 4 minutes remove from heat and let the mixture sit 5 minutes or so to cool slightly. Stir in the vanilla and ladle into hot jars. Wipe rims, seal, and process in a water bath canner for 10 minutes.

Makes 7 half-pint jars.

LIME MARMALADE

4 limes

1 pound pears (about 2 large)

4 cups water

¼ cup bottled lemon juice

6 cups sugar

¼ teaspoon salt

Peel the limes—I used a lemon zester for this recipe. If you don't have a lemon zester, then just peel the limes and cut the peel into thin slices. Put the peel into a saucepan with water to cover and boil for 15 minutes. Drain and repeat. Remove the white flesh from the limes and cut the pulp into thin slices. Remove the seeds and membranes. Put the peel and pulp into a heavy pan. Now peel, core, and tiny dice the pears. Add the pears to the lime and add water, lemon juice, sugar, and salt. Stir over high heat until sugar is dissolved. Turn the heat down and cook over low heat, stirring occasionally, until the marmalade reaches the jell point. Remove from heat and let the marmalade sit for 5 minutes. If any foam has formed skim it off with a metal spoon. Stir and ladle into hot jars, wipe rims, seal, and process in a water bath canner for 10 minutes.

Makes 5 to 6 half-pints.

ORANGE-PINEAPPLE MARMALADE

I like to add one jar of this to my fruitcake recipe. It gives your fruitcake a beautiful shine when it's done.

peel of 3 oranges

pulp of 6 oranges

2 cans (20 ounces each) crushed pineapple (do not drain)

¼ cup bottled lemon juice

5 cups sugar

½ teaspoon ground ginger

Peel three oranges. Put peel in a saucepan with 1 cup of water and boil 40 minutes. Remove from heat and drain. Slice into slivers. Peel other oranges, remove white flesh, and slice orange pulp, removing seed and membrane. Put peel, pulp, undrained pineapple, lemon juice, sugar, and ginger into a pan. Bring to a boil over high heat, stirring constantly to dissolve sugar. Continue cooking over medium heat, stirring occasionally until the marmalade thickens and turns a beautiful amber color. Remove from heat and let sit to cool 5 to 7 minutes. Remove any foam that has formed. Ladle into hot jars, wipe rims, seal, and process in a water bath canner for 10 minutes.

Makes 6 half-pints.

© Steven Mark Needham/Envision

CONSERVES

Conserves are much like jams and preserves. They usually combine one or more fruits and contain nuts and raisins or other diced fruits.

© Brian Leatart

FIG CONSERVE

3 pounds figs or 4½ cups puree

½ cup bottled lemon juice

4 cups sugar

½ cup slivered almonds

1 teaspoon vanilla

Peel figs and mash. Put figs, lemon juice, sugar, almonds, and vanilla into a heavy saucepan. Stirring, bring mixture to a slow boil. Boil slowly and stir often until the mixture thickens and becomes transparent. Remove from heat and skim off any foam that has formed. Leave off heat for 5 minutes and then ladle into hot jars. Wipe rims, seal, and process in a water bath canner for 10 minutes.

Makes 6 to 7 half-pints.

PLUM-APPLE CONSERVE

3½ pounds plums (about 20 medium-size)

1½ cups water

4 tablespoons bottled lemon juice

2 pounds apples (about 6 medium-size)

¾ cup slivered almonds

½ cup golden raisins

1 package (2 ounces) powdered fruit pectin

8 cups sugar

Wash and pit plums. Put in a saucepan with ½ cup water and 2 tablespoons lemon juice. Cook for 10 minutes. Puree in a food mill or a food processor. Peel, core, and slice apples and cook them in a pan with 1 cup water and 2 tablespoons of lemon juice. Cook for about 20 minutes. Puree apples. Combine purees, almonds, and raisins, and bring to a boil. Add pectin and stir to blend, bring back to a boil and add sugar all at once. Stirring constantly, bring mixture back to a rolling boil and boil for 1 minute. Remove from heat, skimming any foam that has formed. Ladle into hot jars, wipe rims, and seal. Process for 10 minutes in a water bath canner.

Makes 6 half-pint jars.

CHERRY-BLUEBERRY CONSERVE

3½ cups cherries

3½ cups blueberries

Peel from 1 orange

4½ cups sugar

1 cup walnuts, chopped

Pit cherries and cut in half. Wash blueberries and, if large, whirl in the food processor once or twice. Put the fruit into a heavy saucepan, then add orange peel and sugar. Heat mixture until sugar dissolves. Add walnut bits and bring mixture to a slow boil. Cook for 20 to 30 minutes or until the mixture begins to thicken and reaches the jell point (which is 220°F at sea level). Remove from heat, skim off any foam that has formed. Ladle into hot jars, wipe rims, and seal. Process for 10 minutes in a water bath canner.

Makes 7 to 8 half-pint jars.

© Bill Margerin/FPG International

LEMON-CRANBERRY CONSERVE

This is a great tasting conserve, especially if you like lemon. The blend of flavors and textures is nice. I love black walnuts so I used them because of their distinct flavor, but if you can't find them, any regular walnut will do. Almonds are also nice.

1 pound cranberries

1 cup water

zest of 2 lemons

pulp of 2 lemons

6 cups sugar

¾ cup lemonade concentrate

1 cup dried apples

1 cup black walnuts

Wash cranberries and put into a heavy saucepan with 1 cup water, lemon zest, lemon pulp, sugar, and lemonade concentrate. Bring to a boil, stirring constantly. Remove from stove and let mixture sit 30 minutes. Chop dried apples and add to cranberry mixture after it has sat for 30 minutes. Return mixture to a boil and add chopped walnuts. Boil the mixture slowly, stirring occasionally until it becomes thick and shiny. Remove conserve and let sit 5 minutes, skimming foam if necessary. Ladle into hot jars, wipe rims, seal jars, and process in a water bath canner for 10 minutes.

Makes 7 to 8 half-pint jars.

BUTTERS

Butters are fruit purees that can be made with one or more fruits. They are cooked slowly until they are of a good spreading consistency. You can add any spices you want to and you can use white or brown sugar. Brown sugar will darken the butter, but it gives it a nice flavor.

You can cook fruit butter on top of the stove, in a slow oven, or in a crockpot. I prefer cooking mine in the oven only because I can busy myself around the house and keep an eye on it while it cooks. Meanwhile, my house smells wonderful. Make sure you stir often so you don't end up burning it on the bottom or edges.

© Stan Sholik/FPG International

APRICOT BUTTER

4 pounds apricots or 8 cups puree

½ cup water

3 tablespoons bottled lemon juice

4 cups sugar

1 teaspoon cinnamon

¼ teaspoon ground allspice

¼ teaspoon nutmeg

¼ teaspoon salt

Clean and pit apricots. Put apricots, water, and lemon juice in a saucepan and cook for 15 to 20 minutes until apricots are soft. Remove the apricots and puree in a food mill, food processor, or with the strainer attachment to the Cuisinart. Put puree in a heavy pan and add sugar, cinnamon, allspice, nutmeg, and salt. Bring to a boil, stirring, until all sugar is dissolved. When sugar is dissolved put the mixture into a roasting pan. Put in a 300°F oven and cook until thick and clear, about 1½ to 2½ hours. Stir often or it will burn on the bottom and sides. The butter is done when a sample is put on a plate and there is no rim of liquid around it. When done, ladle into hot jars, wipe rims, and seal. Process in a water bath canner for 10 minutes.

Makes 5 to 6 half-pint jars.

LOQUAT BUTTER

I love the tart taste of this butter spread on a sweet bread.

4 pounds loquats

¾ cup bottled lemon juice

1 cup water

1 lemon, cut in half

2 whole sticks cinnamon

3 cups sugar

Wash loquats, remove stem and flower ends, remove seeds, and cut in half. Put cut fruit into a heavy saucepan with the lemon juice and water. Add halved lemon and the whole cinnamon sticks. Bring to a boil, stirring occasionally, and cook for 30 minutes. Remove the lemon and cinnamon sticks. Continue cooking until mushy. Use a food mill or food processor, and puree. Put the puree into a heavy pan and add sugar. Stir occasionally for 15 to 20 minutes until the puree is thick and spreadable. Put into hot jars, clean rims, and seal. If you like a tart butter add 1 cup less sugar. Process in a water bath canner for 10 minutes.

Makes 4 half-pint jars.

CARRIE'S FAVORITE APPLE BUTTER

6 pounds apples

1 cup water

¼ cup bottled lemon juice

3 cups granulated sugar

3 cups light brown sugar

½ cup apple shnapps liquor

1 teaspoon cinnamon

½ teaspoon nutmeg

¼ teaspoon ground allspice

¼ teaspoon ground cloves

¼ teaspoon salt

1 teaspoon vanilla

Peel, core, and slice apples into water containing ascorbic acid, until all fruit is prepared. Drain the fruit and cook the apples with 1 cup water, in a heavy, covered saucepan, for 10 to 15 minutes. When apples are soft, process until smooth or grind in a food mill. Put puree in a heavy pan and add lemon juice, granulated and brown sugars, liquor, the spices, salt, and vanilla. Stir well to blend and heat to a boil, stirring to dissolve the sugars. Turn heat to low and continue to cook until very thick and spreadable. Stir occasionally so the butter doesn't burn on the bottom or sides. To test if butter is done, put a spoonful on a plate and make sure there is no liquid around the edges. When done, ladle into jars, clean rims, seal, and process in a water bath canner for 10 minutes.

Makes 4 pints and 1 half-pint.

PLUM-APPLE BUTTER

2½ pounds plums (about 15)

½ cup bottled lemon juice

1 cup water

2½ pounds apples (about 5)

5½ cups sugar

1 teaspoon cinnamon

¼ teaspoon ground cloves

¼ teaspoon nutmeg

½ teaspoon salt

Wash, then depending on size, cut plums in halves or quarters. Remove pits. Cook with ¼ cup of the lemon juice and ½ cup of the water for 20 to 30 minutes. Stir often so they do not burn. When soft, puree in a food mill or with the strainer attachment to the Cuisinart. Peel, core, and slice apples. Cook apples, ¼ cup lemon juice, and ½ cup water in a covered pan. Cook for 10 minutes or until apples are soft. Puree apples in a food mill or food processor. Combine purees, sugar, spices, and salt. Cook, stirring constantly until mixture boils and sugar dissolves. Put mixture in a heavy roasting pan and put into a 300°F oven. Stir occasionally so it does not burn on the bottom or sides. Continue cooking until thick. Test by putting some on a saucer—if no liquid is on the edges it is done. Ladle into hot jars, clean rims, and seal. Process in a water bath canner for 10 minutes.

Makes 6 to 7 half-pint jars.

CHAPTER FOUR

CANNING VEGETABLES

INTRODUCTION TO VEGETABLES

Summer is here and our gardens are overflowing with vegetables. I love a vegetable garden and can hardly wait for spring to start mine. But when my family says they have seen enough peas or beans for awhile, I know it is time to start canning this bounty so we can enjoy them later in the year when fresh vegetables are only a memory.

Vegetables are best canned as fresh as possible, before they start losing their flavor and nutritional value. You want your vegetables crisp not limp, or you won't have a good finished product.

All vegetables except tomatoes require high temperatures because of their low-acid content. To reach this high of a temperature you must use steam under pressure. That is why we use a pressure canner. The only time vegetables are processed in a boiling water canner is if vinegar is used in the recipe. You will find several vegetables in my pickling chapter.

If you carefully follow directions and the timing schedules (making altitude adjustments where necessary), your food should be safe. But as you open each jar make sure you hear the pop of a good seal and that the food looks and smells good. Some food poisoning toxins are not easily detected. So if you are using vegetables someone else has canned and you are not sure just how well they followed directions, it would be a good idea to boil the vegetables for 15 to 20 minutes before serving. Never hesitate to discard vegetables about which you have the slightest doubt—food poisoning can be fatal.

THE PRESSURE CANNER

A pressure canner is a metal kettle and cover that are clamped together to make them steam tight. It will have a weight gauge from 5 pounds to 15 pounds, a vent or petcock, and a safety gauge. To safely work your pressure canner always follow the directions given with your canner. Also, always check to see that the safety valve opening and petcock are clean. Hold up the lid and look through the safety valve and make sure you see through it. If you can't, run a string through the hole and clean it. You may have to do this several times during the canning season.

Make sure you have a rack in the bottom of the canner so the steam can circulate. If you are processing half-pints or pints you can use a normal-size pressure cooker and not buy the large one.

© Robert Edwards

PROCESSING TIMES AT 15 POUNDS PER SQUARE INCH AT VARIOUS ALTITUDES FOR PINT AND QUART MASON JARS PROCESSED IN 12-, 16-, OR 21-QUART PRESSURE CANNERS (HOT OR COLD PACK PROCEDURE).		
	PROCESSING TIME (MINUTES) AT ALTITUDES—	
PRODUCT*	Less than 3,000 feet	3,000 to 7,000 feet	Over 7,000 feet
Asparagus	15	25	35
Beans, lima	30	60	85
Beans, snap or wax	15	30	45
Beets, whole or sliced	15	30	45
Carrots	15	30	45
Corn, whole kernel	50	90	135
Mushrooms	20	40	60
Okra	15	30	45
Parsnips	15	30	45
Peas, green	30	60	85
Peas, black-eye	30	60	85
Potatoes, new-whole	20	40	60
Rutabagas, sliced or diced	30	60	85
Squash, cubed	20	40	60
Sweet potatoes	50	90	135
Turnips, cubed	15	30	45

*Processing times at 15 pounds per square inch have not been established for all vegetables.
University of California, Davis; Department of Food Technology

STEP-BY-STEP PROCEDURES FOR CANNING VEGETABLES

CHECK AND CLEAN ALL EQUIPMENT: Check jars and lids for nicks and cracks and wash them in hot, soapy water. Sterilize jars by boiling and have them hot before filling them with food. Always check to see that you have new flat metal lids before you start canning.

PREPARE YOUR FOOD: Use very fresh, crisp vegetables. Wash vegetables carefully, using a vegetable brush when needed. Cut food according to the directions given in the recipe. Precook or blanch your vegetables. You may want to raw-pack asparagus and whole beans because they will retain their shape and color better.

FILLING THE JARS: If you have precooked the vegetables you can use the cooking liquid for the canning liquid. If you have not precooked the vegetables use boiling water for the canning liquid. You can add salt to jars or, if you are on a salt-free diet, omit it. The salt will enhance the taste of your vegetables. Add salt to your jar, fill with boiling liquid (look at the vegetable chart for each vegetable to see how much headspace to leave). Release any air bubbles and add more liquid if needed. Wipe the rims clean and seal.

PROCESSING PROCEDURES: Look at the recipe or table to see timing and at what weight to process vegetables. Make sure you check the time for the size of jar you are using. Always read the directions given with your pressure canner.

Add 2 to 3 inches of boiling water in the canner. Make sure the rack is in place and add the jars to the canner. Clamp on the lid following manufacturer's directions and vent the canner by leaving the petcock open or the vent pipe uncovered and let a stream of steam escape for at least 10 minutes. After venting, close the petcock or put on a weighted gauge and bring the canner to the right pressure. Start timing when the pressure is correct and process for the length of time in each recipe. Regulate the heat to keep it at the right pressure. Don't let the pressure fall.

After processing remove the canner from the heat (do not tilt) and wait until the pressure drops to zero. Open the petcock and remove the weighted gauge. Be very careful not to burn yourself with steam. Open the canner, lifting the side facing away from you and let the steam out slowly and then, carefully, totally remove the lid.

Leave the jars in the kettle until they cool a little (15 to 20 minutes). Then remove them with a jar lifter to a draft-free place to cool completely. When cool test for seal and store in a cool, dry, dark place.

PROBLEMS YOU MAY HAVE WITH VEGETABLES	
Loss of liquid.	Jars are too full or you did not leave enough headspace. Also with a pressure canner, the pressure rate can cause this problem. This does not mean that the food is necessarily spoiled.
Foods change color.	The vegetable was overcooked or the liquid in the jar did not cover the food.
Mold on food.	The jar was not sealed or the seal was not tight enough and food has spoiled. **Throw out the food.**
Cloudy vegetables.	Hard water (if your area has hard water you can use bottled water) or you used vegetables which were too old. The vegetables may be spoiled; check for a bad smell and throw out.
Sediment on bottom of jar.	Hard water used or table salt used.
Discolored lid on jar.	Caused by certain compounds found in foods. The food is still good. The discoloration is harmless.

HOW TO PREPARE VEGETABLES FOR CANNING

VEGETABLES	HOW TO PREPARE	PROCESSING TIME (10 pounds pressure)	
		PINT	QUART
		minutes	
ARTICHOKES	Use small artichokes. Trim to 1¼ to 2 inches in length. Pre-cook 5 minutes in water to which ¾ cup of vinegar per gallon has been added. Drain. Pack hot into hot jars. Do not overfill. Cover with a boiling brine prepared by adding ¾ cup vinegar or lemon juice and 3 tablespoons salt to 1 gallon water. Fill to within ¾ inch of tops of pint or quart jars. Seal.	25	25
ASPARAGUS	Sort, wash, and cut in lengths ¾ inch shorter than the jar or cut into 1- or 2- inch pieces. Cut off scales (bracts). Pre-cook in boiling water for 1 to 3 minutes to wilt. Then plunge quickly into cold water. **To pack whole:** Gather a bundle of stalks with the ends down and fill jar. Do not pack tightly. Add ½ teaspoon salt for pints, 1 teaspoon salt for quarts. Cover with boiling water to ¾ inch of top of jar. Seal. **To pack cuts:** Fill to ¾ inch from top of jar with cuts. Add ½ teaspoon salt for pints, 1 teaspoon salt for quarts. Cover with boiling water to within ¾ inch of top of jar. Seal.	28 28	32 32
BEANS, FRESH LIMA	**To pack hot:** Proceed as directed for peas. Process as directed for lima beans. **To pack raw:** Use ½ teaspoon salt for pint jars; 1 teaspoon salt for quart jars. **Small beans:** Pack pint jars loosely to within 1 inch of tops; quarts to 1¼ inches. **Large beans:** Pack pint jars loosely to within ¾ inch of tops; quarts to 1¾ inches. Add salt. Fill to ¾ inch of top with boiling water. Seal.	40	50
BEANS, STRING	Sort and snip off string if necessary. Use ½ teaspoon salt for pint jars; 1 teaspoon salt for quart jars. For mature beans, see *Peas, mature.* **To pack hot:** Cut in 1-to 1½-inch lengths. Pre-cook in boiling water until pliable, about 2 to 5 minutes. Pack hot into hot jars. Add salt. Cover to within ¾ inch of jar tops with the boiling liquid in which the beans were pre-cooked. Add boiling water if needed. Seal. If beans are left whole, pack beans standing on ends. Seal. **To pack raw:** Cut into 1-inch pieces. Pack tightly to within ¾ inch of jar tops. Add salt. Cover with boiling water to within ¾ inch of top. Seal.	20 25 20	25 30 25
BEETS	**To pack hot:** Leave on roots and 1 to 1½ inch of stems. Boil until skins slip off (about 15 minutes). Dip in cold water. Peel, trim, and slice. Discard woody beets. Reheat in small amount of water. Pack hot into hot jars. Add ½ teaspoon salt to pint jars; 1 teaspoon salt to quart jars. Cover to within ½ inch of jar tops with the boiling liquid in which the beets were reheated. Add boiling water if needed. Seal. *Raw packing of beets is not recommended.*	35	40

VEGETABLES	HOW TO PREPARE	PROCESSING TIME (10 pounds pressure)	
		PINT	QUART
		minutes	
CARROTS	**To pack raw:** Wash and scrape or peel. Pack cold, sliced, or asparagus style to within 1 inch of tops of pint or quart jars. Add ½ teaspoon salt to pint jars; 1 teaspoon salt to quart jars. Add boiling water to within ¾ inch of top. Seal.	30	30
CELERY	Prepare and slice. Use ½ teaspoon salt for pint jars; 1 teaspoon for quart jars. **To pack hot:** Pre-cook 1 to 3 minutes depending on size and tenderness. Pack hot into hot jars. Add salt. Cover to within ¾ inch of jar tops with boiling liquid in which the celery was pre-cooked. Add boiling water if needed. Seal. **To pack raw:** Slice or cut asparagus style. Pack loosely to within ¾ inch of jar tops. Add salt. Cover with boiling water to within ¾ inch of tops. Seal.	35 30	35 30
CORN, WHOLE KERNEL	**To pack hot:** Can very soon after harvest. Use a sharp knife to cut raw corn from cob at two-thirds of the total depth of the kernels. Do not scrape the cobs. Cover well with brine (1 level tablespoon salt to 1 quart water). Heat to boiling point. Pack hot into hot jars to within 1 inch of jar tops. Seal. *Raw pack is not recommended.*	55	70
CORN, CREAM STYLE	**To pack hot:** Prepare as for whole kernel corn, but scrape the cobs (do not scrape off any of the cob material). Proceed as directed for whole kernel corn. Leave 1½ inch headspace. Seal. *Quart jars are not recommended.* *Raw pack is not recommended.*	85	not rec.
CORN, HOMINY	Cover hominy well with brine, as directed for whole kernel corn. Heat to boiling point. Pack hot into hot jars to within 1 inch of tops. Seal. *Raw pack is not recommended.*	75	90
GREENS	Spinach, swiss chard, beet greens, other greens. *Home canning is not recommended.*	15	15
MUSHROOMS	NOTE: Trim stems and discolored parts. Rinse in cold water. Leave small mushrooms whole; cut larger ones into halves or quarters. Blanch in simmering hot water or steam for 4 minutes. Pack hot mushrooms into hot jars. Add ½ teaspoon salt and ½ teaspoon of lemon juice to pints. Add boiling cooking liquid or water to cover mushrooms, leaving ½ inch headspace. *Mushrooms will be overcooked if processed enough to be safe.* Apply lids and ring bands.	30	Don't use
OKRA	**To pack hot:** Use young, tender pods. Wash and trim. Leave pods whole or cut into 1-inch pieces. Boil for 1 minute. Pack hot into hot jars, leaving 1 inch headspace. Add ½ teaspoon salt to pints, 1 teaspoon to quarts. Add boiling water to 1 inch of top. Seal.	25	40

VEGETABLES	HOW TO PREPARE	PROCESSING TIME (10 pounds pressure)	
		PINT	QUART
		minutes	
ONIONS, SMALL WHITE	Follow directions for artichokes.		
PEAS, FRESH GREEN	**To pack hot:** Can only young, tender peas. Hull and pre-cook for 1 to 4 minutes in a small amount of water until the skins wrinkle. Pack hot into hot jars to within 1¼ inches of tops. Add salt. Cover to within 1 inch of jar tops with the boiling liquid in which the peas were cooked. Add boiling water if needed. Seal.	40	45
	To pack raw: Pack loosely to within 1 inch of jar tops. Add ½ teaspoon salt for pint jars; 1 teaspoon salt for quart jars. Cover with boiling water to within 1 inch of top. Seal.	40	45
PEAS, FRESH BLACK-EYE	**To pack hot:** Follow directions for green peas. *Raw pack is not recommended.*	50	55
PEPPERS, BELL-GREEN, RED, AND PIMENTO	**To pack hot:** Cut out the stem end of each pepper, and remove the core and seeds. Peel peppers by heating in a gas flame or roasting in a very hot oven until the skins separate. Chill at once in cold water. Pack into jars. Cover with boiling water to within ½ inch of jar tops. Add ½ teaspoon salt to pint jars; 1 teaspoon salt to quart jars. It is also necessary to add 1½ teaspoons bottled lemon juice to pint jars; 1 tablespoon lemon juice to each quart jar. *(Process at only 5 pounds pressure; higher pressures affect texture and flavor.)* Seal.	(5 lb pressure) 50	60
POTATOES, NEW	Peel new potatoes. Leave small ones whole; cut larger ones in halves. Pack cold without pre-cooking. Add boiling brine made with 1½ to 2 tablespoons salt to 1 quart water. Fill to within ¾ to 1 inch of jar tops. Seal.	35	40
POTATOES, SWEET	Wash and remove any blemishes. **To pack dry:** Place in steamer over boiling water or boil in a small amount of water until crisp-tender. Peel and cut into pieces. Pack tightly into jars, pressing to fill spaces. Add no salt or liquid. Apply lids and ring bands.	65	95
	To pack wet: Steam or boil as for dry pack, but remove as soon as skins slip off easily. Peel, cut into pieces, and pack into jars to within 1 inch of tops. Add ½ teaspoon salt to quarts. Cover with boiling water or a syrup of 1 part sugar to 2 parts water, leaving ¾ inch headspace. Apply lids and ringbands.	55	90
PUMPKIN OR MATURE SQUASH, CUBED	**To pack hot:** Wash, remove seeds, and peel. Cut into 1-inch cubes. Add enough water to cover; bring to a boil. Pack hot cubes to ½ inch of the top. Add ½ teaspoon salt to pints; 1 teaspoon to quarts. Cover with hot cooking liquid, leaving ½ inch headspace. Seal. *Raw pack is not recommended.*	55	90

University of California, Davis; Department of Food Technology.

VEGETABLES	HOW TO PREPARE	PROCESSING TIME (10 pounds pressure)	
		PINT	QUART
		minutes	
PUMPKIN OR MATURE SQUASH, STRAINED	Scrape out fibrous material and cut flesh and rind into strips. Boil in water, or steam, until flesh is soft. Scrape flesh from rind and press through a colander. Bring to a boil. Pack hot into hot jars to within ¾ to 1 inch of tops. Add ½ teaspoon salt to pint jars; 1 teaspoon salt to quart jars. Seal. *Raw pack is not recommended.*	85	115
SQUASH, SUMMER CROOKNECK, ZUCCHINI, PATTYPAN	*Canning summer squash produces a soft to mushy product.* Wash and trim ends; do not peel. Cut into ½-inch thick slices. **To pack hot:** Put into a pan, add water to just cover, and bring to boiling. Pack hot into hot jars, filling loosely up to jar shoulders. Add ½ teaspoon salt to pints, 1 teaspoon to quarts. Cover with boiling cooking liquid, leaving ½ inch headspace. Apply lids and ring bands.	30	40
	To pack raw: Pack slices tightly into jars to within 1 inch of tops. Add salt as for hot pack, then fill jars with boiling water, leaving ½ inch headspace. Apply lids and ring bands.	25	30
TURNIPS	Follow directions for carrots.		

ASPARAGUS

11 pounds asparagus (about 200 stalks)

1 garlic clove

1 piece red bell pepper, ½ inch long

½ teaspoon salt

Wash and cut asparagus ¾ inch shorter than your jar. Scrape off scales. Put garlic clove, bell pepper, and salt into hot jars. Loosely pack asparagus, stem end down. Add boiling water, leaving ½-inch headspace. Release air bubbles, wipe rims, and seal. Process in a pressure canner at 10 pounds. Pints take 30 minutes and quarts take 40 minutes.

Makes 7 pints.

GREEN BEANS TIED WITH CARROTS

These look so pretty in the jar and make a really nice gift. Tell whoever is the recipient of these beans to remove them carefully from the jar. A bundle of these drizzled with dressing placed on the side of a chicken salad makes a very impressive sight.

5½ pounds beans

2 to 3 carrots

½ teaspoon salt for pints or ¾ teaspoon salt for quarts

Pick beautiful small beans. Wash and remove stem end and string if necessary. Cook beans in boiling water for 3 to 4 minutes. Do not cover pan— the beans will stay greener. Plunge beans into cold water. Use the deepest orange carrots you can find. Wash and peel carrots. Using a vegetable peeler, peel strips of carrot lengthwise. Cook in boiling water until carrots bend easily but do not break. Take 5 to 6 beans and wrap one piece of carrot around the beans. Repeat this until all beans are used. Take hot jars and add salt. Lay jars on their sides and put several bundles of beans in each jar. Don't pack too tightly. Stand jars up and add boiling water to within ¾ inch of the top of the jar. Carefully remove air bubbles, clean rims, and seal. Process in a pressure canner at 10 pounds, 30 minutes for quarts, 25 minutes for pints.

Makes 6 to 7 pints.

MIXED VEGETABLES

This is very pretty in the jar. Drain the vegetables and sauté them in a little unsalted butter and sprinkle with veggie salt. Veggie salt can be found in the health food section of your grocery store; it lends a great flavor to many foods. Try it on oven-fried potatoes or on any other vegetable. You can also cover these vegetables with cheese sauce and warm them in the oven. These make for a fast special vegetable dish.

4 cups red bell pepper, cut in 1½-inch pieces

4 cups yellow bell pepper, cut in 1½-inch pieces

2 pounds green beans, stem end cut and bean stringed, if necessary

4 cups carrots cut on the diagonal in ¼-inch slices

3 cans (8 ounces each) water chestnuts

In each jar: 1 teaspoon salt, one slice yellow onion

Wash and prepare vegetables. Boil water in a large pan and dip peppers in for 2 minutes (just to soften). Use an 8 to 10 quart pot or larger with a strainer in it or a large pan a strainer will fit in. This will let you use the same water for all vegetables. Remove peppers and add beans; parboil for 5 minutes. Drain beans. Cook carrots in water for 3 minutes; drain. Drain the water chestnuts. To each hot jar add salt and one slice of onion. Carefully add vegetables with water chestnuts, layering them so they look pretty in the jar. Fill the jar with boiling water to within ½ inch of the top. Release air bubbles and seal. Process in a pressure canner at 10 pounds for 30 minutes for quarts, 10 pounds for 25 minutes for pints.

Makes 4 to 5 quarts or 8 to 10 pints.

© Photri

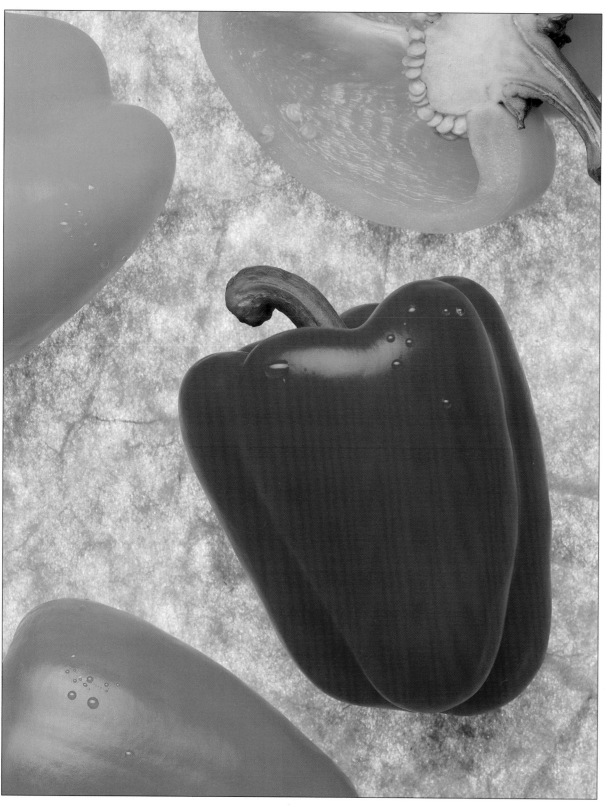

© Amy Reichman/Envision

MELANGE OF PEPPERS

These peppers can be served warm with grilled chicken breast and warm flour tortillas.

8 green bell peppers

8 red peppers

8 yellow peppers

In each jar:

1 teaspoon salt

1 clove garlic

a sprig of fresh tarragon

2 tablespoons tarragon vinegar

Roast peppers in a 400°F oven, turning frequently until they are partially brown and start to bubble. Remove from oven and peel. Cut peppers open and remove white membrane and seeds. Cut each pepper lengthwise into six strips and then in half. Mix peppers for color and interest. Using an 8 to 10 quart pot (the kind with a strainer inside) or a pan large enough to hold a strainer, boil water and add peppers for 2 to 3 minutes, just long enough to soften slightly, so the peppers will fit into the jars more easily. Plunge immediately into cold water to stop the cooking. Put 1 teaspoon salt, 1 clove garlic, a sprig of fresh tarragon, and tarragon vinegar into each hot jar. Fill jar with boiling water, leaving ½-inch headspace. Remove air bubbles, clean rims, and seal. Process in a pressure canner at 10 pounds, for 35 minutes.

Makes 5 to 6 quarts.

CARROTS WITH MINT

8 pounds baby carrots

In each jar:

1 clove garlic

1 sprig mint, about 2 inches long

1 teaspoon lemon juice

½ teaspoon salt

Wash and scrape carrots. Put 1 garlic clove, a sprig of mint, 1 teaspoon lemon juice, and ½ teaspoon salt in each pint. Add carrots and fill jar with boiling water to within ½ inch of tops of jars. Release air bubbles, clean rims, and seal. Process in a pressure canner at 10 pounds for 30 minutes.

Makes 5 to 6 pints.

CHAPTER FIVE

PICKLES, RELISHES, AND CHUTNEYS

Fruits and vegetables can become crisp, tangy, sweet and sour, or sour with the process of pickling. The flavor changes easily by varying the amount of vinegar, salt, sugar, or seasonings. That is the fun of making these products at home. You can have things as spicy or as mild as you want. You must taste as you go through the recipe so it becomes distinctively yours. Then serve with meat, fish, or poultry, or as an accompaniment to curry.

TYPES OF PICKLES

Vegetable Pickles: I have given a few quick pickle recipes using vinegar and salt brines. The favorite vegetable for pickling is the cucumber and the small variety is the most favorable. Do not use waxed cucumbers from your market; you won't like the result. I have also used beans, asparagus, and beets.

Fruits are also wonderful pickled. I use a spicy, sweet-sour syrup. Cloves and cinnamon are common spices used with fruit. You can use many different fruits, but the more popular fruits to pickle are peaches, crabapples, figs, plums, pears, and apples.

Relishes are also included in the pickling chapter because we use vinegar and spices and blend different vegetables and fruit to make a piquant blend.

Chutneys are another type of relish, again using a variety of chopped fruit and vegetables and blending them with seasonings like onion, garlic, ginger, and turmeric.

EQUIPMENT FOR PICKLING

If you have canning equipment you are set for pickling. You want to be careful to use containers made of glass, enamel, high-grade plastic, or stainless steel. Other utensils may chemically react with the brine mixture or high-acid solutions.

You will need colanders, long spoons, cheesecloth for packaging spices, and a food grinder or a food processor. The processor will slice your pickling vegetables perfectly and chop your vegetables for relishes or chutneys in no time. You will need jars and lids that are in good shape and new flat metal lids. Pickles, relishes, and chutneys are processed in a water bath because of the high acidity of all these products, so you will need a water canner or a large pan that will hold enough water to cover the jars with water by 2 inches.

INGREDIENTS FOR PICKLING

Choose firm, fresh vegetables and fruits. Put up as soon as possible after picking or purchasing. The small pickling cucumber is best to use for making crisp pickles. The salad varieties are not as crisp and, if used, it is best to cut them into chunks or slices.

Fruit is best when it is slightly underripe. It will hold its shape better. Try to pick uniformly-sized fruit.

Pickling salt, called for in some of the recipes, can be found in most grocery stores in the summer. Look for it next to ice-cream-making salt.

Fresh spices are preferred and lend wonderful flavor, but dried pickling spices and other ground spices are fine to use.

Granulated beet sugar or brown sugar can both be used. Brown sugar will give a darker color syrup and a little stronger flavor. You may also use half sugar and half honey for sweetness.

Another ingredient so important to the outcome of good crisp pickles is the water. Soft water is great, but hard water can make your pickles cloudy. Hard water will not affect the taste, but if you want you can boil hard water or use distilled water.

Vinegar is one of the main ingredients used in pickling. Pick a good standard vinegar, 40 to 60 grains strength, that is free from sediment. Cider and distilled wine vinegars are good choices. Never overboil vinegar solutions or you may lose the acidity essential for pickling.

Powdered alum is sometimes used to make pickles crispy. But if you have fresh, firm produce and follow directions closely you really don't need it. If you must use it, don't exceed ⅛ teaspoon per quart of liquid plus pickles. Alum can cause digestive problems, so be very careful.

I use pickling lime in a few recipes. You can purchase it from your local nursery. It will not hurt you, but make sure you rinse the food you use it on very well. It makes really nice crisp pickles.

© Burke/Triolo

A FEW PICKLING RULES

You can have a great time with your ingredients when making pickles, relish, or chutney. But make very sure that you follow directions correctly. If you speed up some processes, like adding your vinegar and sugar syrup to the pickles before the brine solution has worked, you will end up with tough, shriveled pickles. Also, the wrong brine solution can work against you. If the brine is too weak it will give you soft pickles and if too strong it will wilt the pickles.

You must also be careful to follow vinegar amounts. You can choose which kinds but not how much or you may end up with an unsafe product.

PROCESSING YOUR PICKLES, RELISHES, AND CHUTNEYS

All pickles, relishes, and chutneys are processed in a boiling water canner. Processing time will vary, but each recipe states the proper time required. If you wish to omit the boiling processing step you can keep your goods refrigerated for a few weeks, but not much longer. Surface yeast or mold is the most common problem of refrigerated foods.

Check your jars and lids to make sure that they are safe to use. Wash in hot, soapy water. Make sure you have new flat metal lids and follow manufacturer's directions on preparing them for use.

Put your food into the hot jars and pour in the liquid to within ½ inch of the rim of the jar. Remove air bubbles and wipe the rim of the jar clean. Seal and place jars in a boiling water bath, adding enough water to cover the jars by 2 inches. Begin counting the processing time when the water returns to a gentle boil. Cool your jars on a wooden block or on folded towels, leaving room for air to circulate around the jars. When the jars are cool test the seal by pressing down on the lid. It should not move. You can then remove the screw band and store in a dark, cool, dry place.

Do not be too anxious to try your wares. The flavor of pickles, relishes, and chutneys all improve when stored for several weeks.

© Michael Grand

COMMON PROBLEMS WITH PICKLES	
Shriveling pickles.	This could be caused by using old vegetables or too strong a vinegar or salt solution. Could also be overprocessed.
Soft or slippery pickles.	You may have used too weak a brine or too little vinegar. Not removing scum as it forms on brine, or using cucumbers with the blossom attached will also make pickles soft.
Hollow pickles.	You probably have old cucumbers. You may have kept them in the brine too long or had faulty growth.
Dark pickles.	Too much spice or cooked too long with spices added. Improper equipment, especially if you used iron.
White sediment on bottom of the jar.	Failure to kill bacteria and spoilage is setting in.
Dull or faded color.	Vegetables are old, or your vinegar is not a good quality or the proper strength (40 to 60 grain is a good strength).

© Christopher Bain

© Amy Reichman/Envision

MARY'S SWEET PICKLES

Mary Allison is a favorite teacher of two of my children, and I think she is just wonderful. My youngest son, T. J., said Mrs. Allison made the best sweet pickles. Well, taste these and see what you think. They are so crisp and have a wonderful flavor. You can get the pickling lime from a garden nursery and it will last you a long time. Be sure you rinse the cucumbers thoroughly after soaking them in the lime.

8 pounds cucumbers

½ cup pickling lime

3 quarts water

2 quarts cider vinegar

9 cups sugar

3 tablespoons salt

2 tablespoons each celery seed, whole cloves, and mixed pickling spices

Wash and slice cucumbers. Soak the cucumbers in lime and water for 24 hours. Then, drain the cucumbers and rinse well. Soak for 3 hours in enough cold water to cover. Drain again and rinse well. Mix the vinegar, sugar, salt, and spices together and pour over the cucumbers. Let stand overnight. In the morning, bring to a boil and boil on low for 35 minutes. Fill hot jars to within ½ inch of the tops, release air bubbles, wipe the rims, and seal.

Makes 6 quarts or 12 half-pints.

SWEET CHIPS

5 pounds small cucumbers

⅓ cup salt

6 cups vinegar

7 to 8 cups sugar

1 tablespoon pickling spice

1½ teaspoons celery seed

¾ teaspoon turmeric

1 whole stick cinnamon

1 teaspoon vanilla (optional)

Wash and slice cucumbers. Put in a non-metallic container and pour enough boiling water to cover. You may want to lay a plate on top of the cucumbers as a weight so all the cucumbers are in the water. Eight hours later, drain cucumbers and cover again with boiling water, adding the salt. The next day drain cucumbers. Make a syrup of 3 cups of the vinegar and 3 cups of the sugar, the pickling spice, celery seed, turmeric, and cinnamon stick.

Bring the syrup to a boil and pour on cucumbers. Let stand 8 hours or overnight. Drain, saving the syrup. Add 2 cups vinegar and 2 cups sugar to syrup and bring to a boil. Pour on pickles and let stand 12 hours. Remove the cinnamon stick, drain, and add 1 cup vinegar and 2 to 3 cups sugar (to taste). Bring to a boil and add vanilla. Pack the pickles in the jars and cover with the boiling syrup to within ½ inch of the top. Remove air bubbles, clean rims, and seal. Process in a water bath canner for 10 minutes.

Makes 7 to 8 12-ounce jars.

BREAD AND BUTTER PICKLES

4 quarts pickling cucumbers (about 6 pounds)

4 large onions

½ cup salt

4 cups vinegar

4 cups sugar

1 tablespoon celery seed

2 teaspoons turmeric

2 tablespoons mustard seed

1 teaspoon mixed pickling spices

Slice cucumbers and onions and alternately layer in a strainer covering each layer with salt. Cover with ice and let drain 3 hours. Add ice as needed. Drain and rinse thoroughly. Combine vinegar, sugar, and spices and bring to a boil. Boil 10 minutes. Add cucumbers and onions and bring to a boil again. Fill hot jars with cucumber and onions. Add hot liquid to within ½ inch of the tops of the jars. Release air bubbles, clean the rims of the jars, and seal. Process in a water bath canner for 10 minutes.

Makes 7 to 8 pints.

BETTY KEECH'S DILL PICKLES

This recipe really reaches back into my past. Until I was seven years old, I lived on a ranch and Betty lived a couple of houses away. According to her daughter, Donna, she would can just about anything she could get her hands on. So I am sharing her recipe for Dill Pickles, which everyone I know feels are the best dill pickles around. Betty never processes her pickles and says they are great even after a year. However, if you want to be assured a seal you can process for 10 minutes. I also tried soaking the pickles in food-grade pickling lime, bought at a local nursery, overnight and had really crispy pickles. Put pickles in 3 quarts of water with ½ cup pickling lime and leave for 24 hours. Rinse the pickles thoroughly and proceed with Betty's recipe.

10 to 12 pounds small cucumbers

1½ gallons vinegar

1½ gallons water

1 cup salt

Put in each jar:

1 clove garlic

1 tablespoon pickling spices

several sprigs of fresh dill and 1 tablespooon dill seed

a pinch of alum (do not use if you used lime)

You can keep your pickles whole or slice them. Wash the pickles and cut stems off if left whole or slice with your food processor. Stir the vinegar, water, and salt, and let it just come to a boil. Have hot jars ready and put in garlic, pickling spices, dill, dill seed, and alum (if you did not use lime). Pack the jars with cucumbers. Ladle the hot vinegar mixture over to within ½ inch of the tops of jars. Remove the air bubbles, wipe the rims of the jars, and seal. Process in a water bath canner for 10 minutes.

Makes 9 to 10 quarts.

© Lynn Karlin

ZUCCHINI PICKLES

These pickles are so tasty and crispy. They also are such a pretty color that they look beautiful on a bed of lettuce with many other vegetables.

6 cups sliced green zucchini

6 cups sliced yellow zucchini

2 large onions

1 each yellow, red, and green peppers

½ cup salt

2 cups sugar

4 cups water

4 cups vinegar

2 tablespoons mustard seed

2 tablespoons celery seed

2 teaspoons turmeric

Wash and cut vegetables. (I slice my onions thin and make the zucchini about ½ inch thick.) Cover zucchini, onion, and peppers with water to which salt has been added. Let stand for 2 hours. Drain and rinse the vegetables. Combine the sugar, water, vinegar, and spices and bring to a boil. When it boils add the vegetables and cook 2 to 3 minutes. Pack vegetables into hot jars and fill with the hot liquid, leaving ½-inch headspace. Release air bubbles, clean rims, and seal. Process in a water bath canner for 10 minutes.

Makes 6 to 7 pints.

PICKLED BEETS

8 pounds beets

2 cups sugar

2 cups water

4 cups cider vinegar

2 whole sticks cinnamon

6 whole allspice

8 whole cloves

2 large onions, sliced thin

1 lemon, sliced thin

Wash beets. Cook until just tender—about 20 minutes—and plunge into cold water and slip off skins. Shred beets. Combine sugar, water, and vinegar. Put spices in a piece of cheesecloth, tie them, and add to the vinegar mixture. Bring the mixture to a boil, then lower heat and simmer for 5 minutes. Remove spices. Fill hot jars with beets and onions. Add a lemon slice to each jar and fill with the hot liquid to within ½ inch of the top of the jar. Release air bubbles, clean rims, seal, and process in a water bath canner for 30 minutes.

Makes 4 pints.

MICHELLE'S PICKLED CARROTS

4 pounds baby carrots

2 quarts water

½ cup salt

4 cups water

4 cups vinegar

2 cups sugar

In each pint:

¼ teaspoon celery seed

3 or 4 peppercorns

1 sprig fresh thyme or ½ teaspoon dried thyme

1 garlic clove

½-inch piece of red pepper

¼ teaspoon mixed pickling spices

2 teaspoons olive oil

Scrape and clean carrots. Remove ends. If you do not have baby carrots, cut long carrots into chunks. Put 2 quarts water and salt into a bowl and stir to dissolve salt. Add carrots. Cover carrots and water with ice. Refrigerate for 2 hours. Rinse the carrots well and drain. Rinse again and drain. Bring water, vinegar, and sugar to a boil. Put spices and oil into each pint jar. Fill jars with carrots and then with boiling liquid to within ½ inch of the top. Release air bubbles, clean rims, and seal. Process in a water bath canner for 20 minutes.

Makes 4 to 5 pints.

DILLY BEANS

If you need a quick salad, these beans are wonderful on red-leaf lettuces. Use the liquid for your dressing.

2 pounds green beans

2½ cups water

2½ cups vinegar

¼ cup salt

In each jar put:

1 garlic clove

⅛ teaspoon dried dill

small sprig of fresh dill

3 or 4 peppercorns

1 bay leaf

¼ teaspoon red pepper flakes

Cut ends off of beans and wash thoroughly. If the beans are small (I prefer small beans) leave them whole, otherwise cut into 1-inch lengths. Bring water, vinegar, and salt to a boil, then add beans and cook 2 minutes. Remove beans to a paper-towel-lined cookie sheet, making sure you save the liquid the beans were cooked in. Add all the spices to each hot jar. If whole, stand the beans in the jars and fill to within ½ inch of the rim with the cooking liquid. Release the air bubbles, clean rims, and seal. Process in a water bath canner for 10 minutes.

Makes 4 pints.

RELISH

Relishes are great fun to make and are not just used for hot dogs anymore. Relish makes a good accompaniment for many meats and fish. Some are so tasty you may just want to eat them by the spoonful. Relishes are made from combinations of fruits, vegetables, spices, and good quality vinegars.

AUNT ROSE'S RELISH

This recipe was given to me by my very good friends, Jeff and Patti Coupe. Frances Coupe, Jeff's 95-year-old grandmother, still makes this relish. I hear Jeff eats it by the spoonful so it must be great. Aunt Rose fits in here somewhere, but when you get recipes that have been passed down for so many years you lose track.

6 ripe red tomatoes, cored and quartered

6 green tomatoes, cored and quartered

5 sweet peppers

3 hot peppers

6 medium onions

1 quart cider vinegar

1 pound brown or granulated sugar

1 tablespoon salt

1 tablespoon cinnamon

1 teaspoon ground allspice

1 teaspoon nutmeg

1 teaspoon ground cloves

Add 2 tablespoons of salt to a large bowl of water and add cored and quartered tomatoes to salted water. Remove seeds and membrane from peppers, quarter, and add them to salted water. Peel and quarter onions and add them to salted water. Drain all the vegetables and grind in a food processor or food grinder. Put into a heavy saucepan and add the vinegar, sugar, salt, and spices. Cook over low heat, stirring occasionally, for 2½ to 3 hours. Ladle into hot jars leaving ½-inch headspace, wipe rims, seal, and process in water bath canner for 15 minutes.

Makes 10 half-pints.

© Steven Mark Needham/Envision

PEPPER RELISH

2 green bell peppers, chopped

2 red peppers, chopped

2 onions, chopped

¾ pound green tomatoes, chopped

3 cups vinegar

1½ cups sugar

1 tablespoon salt

2 teaspoons celery seed

1 teaspoon mustard seed

2 teaspoons turmeric

1 teaspoon tarragon

Prepare peppers, onions, and tomatoes. Put vegetables in a large, heavy saucepan and add the rest of the ingredients. Bring to a boil and cook until slightly thickened. Stir occasionally. Pack into hot jars, wipe rims, and seal. Process in a water bath canner for 10 minutes.

Makes 4 to 5 pints.

CORN RELISH

4 cups corn (about 10 ears, or use canned niblets corn)

1 cup red peppers, chopped

1 cup green peppers, chopped

1 cup celery, chopped

1 cup carrots, shredded

½ cup green onions, chopped

2½ cups vinegar

1½ cups sugar

1½ teaspoons salt

1 teaspoon turmeric

1 tablespoon mustard seed

1 teaspoon white pepper

1 teaspoon celery seed

Cook fresh corn 5 minutes in boiling water. Remove corn and put in cold water. Cut corn from cob. If you use canned corn, rinse and drain. Put corn and all other ingredients into a large saucepan and bring to a boil. Simmer for 5 minutes, stirring constantly. Ladle into hot jars, wipe rims, and seal. Process in a water bath canner for 15 minutes.

Makes 7 to 8 pints.

WILMA'S GREEN RELISH

Wilma Casey is a family friend who says she has wonderful childhood memories of making this relish with her mother. It is really easy to make and takes no time at all if you use a food processor for all the chopping.

4 large onions

½ small head cabbage

4 cups green tomatoes

12 green peppers

6 sweet red peppers

½ cup salt

6 cups sugar

1 tablespoon celery seed

2 tablespoons mustard seed

1½ teaspoons turmeric

4 cups cider vinegar

2 cups water

Coarsely grind all vegetables with the steel blade of your food processor or with a food grinder. Sprinkle vegetables with ½ cup salt and mix well. Let stand overnight. The next day, rinse the vegetables well and drain. Put vegetables into a large, heavy saucepan and add sugar, spices, vinegar, and water. Mix well and bring mixture to a boil. When a boil is reached, turn heat down and simmer for 3 minutes. Ladle into hot jars leaving ½-inch headspace, wipe rims, and seal. Process in a water bath canner for 10 minutes.

Makes 8 to 9 pints.

CHUTNEYS

Chutneys are spicy preserves that combine fruits and vegetables with nuts and dried fruits. They are served with curries and as accompaniments to many other meat, fish, and chicken dishes.

© Michael Grand

MANGO CHUTNEY

2 cups mango, diced

2 cups apple, diced

1 onion, diced

½ cup green pepper, diced

½ cup golden raisins

½ cup sliced almonds

1 cup sugar

1 cup apple cider vinegar

¼ teaspoon ground allspice

¼ teaspoon ground cloves

1 teaspoon cinnamon

½ teaspoon salt

Prepare fruit and vegetables. Put all other ingredients into a large, heavy saucepan. Bring to a boil, stirring constantly. Add fruits and vegetables and cook about 30 minutes or until desired consistency, stirring occasionally. Ladle into hot jars leaving ½-inch headspace. Clean rims of jars and seal. Process in a water bath canner for 10 minutes.

Makes 5 or 6 half-pints.

RUSTY'S CHUTNEY

Rusty Ball is a family friend and this recipe is from her great grandmother's family cookbook. This one goes way back and it is really good.

5 pounds tomatoes, cubed

2 large onions, chopped

½ cup salt

1 pound green apples, peeled and chopped

2 cups cider vinegar

6 cups brown sugar

1 teaspoon cinnamon

1 teaspoon ground cloves

1 teaspoon ground allspice

1 teaspoon white pepper

1 teaspoon ground ginger

1 tablespoon mustard seed

¼ teaspoon cayenne pepper

Prepare tomatoes and onions. Sprinkle with ½ cup of salt and let stand overnight. The next day, rinse and drain the tomatoes and onions. Add all ingredients to a heavy, large saucepan and mix well. Bring to a boil. Reduce heat to a simmer and cook until vegetables are soft and appear clear. Ladle into hot jars, leaving ½-inch headspace, clean rims, and seal. Process in a water bath canner for 10 minutes.

Makes about 7 pints.

APPLE-PEAR CHUTNEY

2 cups pears, diced

3 cups apples, diced

2 cups green tomato, diced

1 medium onion, minced

1 red pepper, minced

3 cups cider vinegar

1½ cups sugar

1½ teaspoons salt

½ teaspoon white pepper

¾ teaspoon cinnamon

¼ teaspoon cayenne pepper

1¼ cups golden raisins

Combine all ingredients in a heavy saucepan and bring to a boil stirring constantly. Reduce heat to a simmer and continue cooking until thickened. Ladle into hot jars, wipe rims, and seal. Process in a water bath canner for 10 minutes.

Makes about 7 pints.

PEACHY GINGER CHUTNEY

Spoon this chutney into a cooked, miniature pumpkin that has been scooped out. This is beautiful alongside your Thanksgiving table.

3½ pounds peaches, diced (about 7 large)

1 large onion, minced

1 yellow pepper, diced

1 hot red pepper, diced

½ cup crystallized ginger, chopped

2 cups cider vinegar

3 cups sugar

1 teaspoon cinnamon

¼ teaspoon ground cloves

¼ teaspoon mace

Prepare fruit and vegetables. Put in a heavy saucepan and add the remaining ingredients. Bring to a boil, stirring constantly. Turn heat to a simmer, and cook until desired consistency. Ladle into hot jars leaving ½-inch headspace, wipe rims, and seal. Process in a water bath canner for 10 minutes.

Makes 4 to 5 half-pints.

© Brian Leatart

VINEGARS, OILS, AND OTHER GOODIES

This section will give you recipes for many of the things you buy in gourmet gift shops. You will be surprised how easy they are to make.

Flavored vinegars and oils are wonderful to cook with and lend themselves to making creative and exciting flavored dishes. Those of you on weight-reducing diets or special medical diets will be surprised at how much flavor these vinegars will add to so many foods. They are great on salads, nice to marinate meat in, and will enhance your vegetables without using butter.

Besides oils and vinegars, you can make ketchup, apple syrup, a wonderful caramel sauce, jerky, and many other delicious treats. I have even included a section on baby foods made using the new strainer attachment that can be bought for the Cuisinart food processor. You won't believe how easy it is to use. I only give recipes for fruit baby food, because it has not yet been determined what a safe processing time would be for pureed vegetables or meat. But if you want to make fresh vegetables or meat for the baby, to be eaten in a couple of days, you can do this and then refrigerate it. It will keep all the gristle and such out of the baby food and just give you the pureed meat.

I hope you will enjoy these and think of many great ways to decorate and present them as gifts. There is nothing more appreciated than something homemade.

VINEGARS

Vinegars are really easy to make and fun to use. You can make them look so beautiful in all the interesting bottles that are available in food shops today.

Make sure you start off with very good vinegar and add spices, fresh herbs, or fruits—even citrus peels. Store the vinegar in a cool dark place for several weeks and then strain it into pretty bottles. Add some fresh herbs, peppers, or peels and it will make a lovely gift.

LEMON-THYME VINEGAR

Try tossing some cooked baby shrimp and scallops in a vinaigrette made with this vinegar. Serve on a bed of bibb and radicchio.

1 quart white wine vinegar

1 bunch fresh thyme

peel of one lemon

2 garlic cloves

6 or 7 whole peppercorns

6 or 7 whole coriander seeds

Heat the vinegar until it boils, but do not boil the vinegar. Put all other ingredients into a big glass container with a tight-fitting lid. Pour in the warm vinegar, seal tightly, and store in a cool, dark place. It is best to leave for at least 2 to 3 weeks. At that time, strain the vinegar into a large container. Then pour it into a decorative bottle through a funnel. Add a few new sprigs of fresh thyme and a lemon peel that you have cut in a spiral.

Makes 1 quart of vinegar.

BLACKBERRY VINEGAR

Use fruit vinegars, a little sweet butter, and salt and pepper to deglaze a pan after sautéeing chicken or pork cutlets.

In this vinegar recipe I use rice vinegar. It is a mild, wonderful vinegar often overlooked. You will find it in the Chinese foods section of your grocery store.

6 cups rice vinegar

¼ cup sugar

2 cups fresh blackberries, mashed

Heat the vinegar and sugar until the sugar dissolves. Do not boil. Pour the vinegar over the mashed berries and cover the glass jar with a tight-fitting lid. Leave in a dark, cool place for 2 to 3 days. Strain through a jelly bag or cheesecloth. Pour into a pretty bottle with a tight fitting top.

Makes 1½ quarts of vinegar.

TARRAGON VINEGAR

8 cups white wine vinegar

1 teaspoon sugar

1 large bunch fresh tarragon

1 large piece of red pepper

½ teaspoon whole black pepper

1 teaspoon celery seed

2 garlic cloves

Warm vinegar and sugar. Add all other ingredients to a large glass jar with a tight-fitting lid. Pour warm vinegar into the jar and put the lid on tight. Store in a dark, cool place for 3 to 4 weeks. Then strain vinegar and put into a bottle with a tight screw top or a tight cork. Add a sprig of fresh tarragon, 1 garlic clove, and a new piece of red pepper. It will look pretty and taste great.

Makes 1½ quarts of vinegar.

© Steven Mark Needham/Envision

DILL VINEGAR

I like to use this vinegar to make a homemade mayonnaise to use on cold salmon. Just eliminate the lemon juice from your mayonnaise recipe and add this vinegar in place of it.

6 cups red wine vinegar

1 teaspoon sugar

½ lemon, quartered, seeds removed

1 bunch fresh dill

2 garlic cloves

1 teaspoon peppercorns

1 teaspoon pepper flakes

1 teaspoon celery seed

½ teaspoon whole mustard seed

Heat red wine vinegar and 1 teaspoon sugar until warm. Put dill and other ingredients into a glass jar. Pour warm vinegar over and put on a tight-fitting lid. Store at room temperature in a dark, cool place for at least 2 weeks. At the end of this time, strain vinegar and put into a decorative bottle with a tight cork or a screw top. Add a fresh garlic clove and a fresh sprig of dill.

Makes 1½ quarts of vinegar.

BASIL VINEGAR

I always have this vinegar on hand for making pasta salad.

6 cups white wine vinegar

¼ of a fresh red pepper

1 cup fresh basil leaves, left whole

2 garlic cloves

½ teaspoon whole mustard seed

½ teaspoon whole white pepper

1 teaspoon celery seed

Heat vinegar, but do not boil. Put all other ingredients into a large glass jar with a tight-fitting lid. Pour warm vinegar into the jar, cover tightly, and set in a dark, cool place for at least 2 weeks. After 2 or more weeks, strain vinegar into a large container. Pour vinegar into pretty bottles, using a funnel to help. Add a new garlic clove and a fresh sprig of basil. Put on a tight cork or screw top.

Makes 1½ quarts of vinegar.

RASPBERRY VINEGAR

Try fruit-flavored vinegars on salads or sprinkle on your favorite cooked vegetables.

3 cups fresh raspberries, mashed

6 cups white wine vinegar

¼ cup sugar

Heat the vinegar and sugar until the sugar dissolves, but do not boil. Pour vinegar over raspberries in a large glass jar. Put in a dark, cool place for 3 or 4 days. Strain the vinegar through a jelly bag so it is very clear. Do not squeeze the bag. Pour through a funnel into a decorative jar and seal with a tight lid or cork.

Makes 7 cups of vinegar.

© Brian Leatart

FLAVORED OILS

Flavored oils are fun to use. If you have ever sautéed chicken in grape oil or used walnut oil on bibb lettuce, you know how good these can be. For the easiest spiced oils pick your favorite oil (be it olive, corn, or any other variety). Add fresh herbs like basil, tarragon, dill, rosemary, or thyme. You can be very imaginative. Just add what you want to a pretty bottle with a tight-fitting top or cork, add oil, and let sit at least two weeks before using. The longer it sits the more pronounced the flavor. Shake the bottle every couple of days to help the flavor spread. Use these oils for sautéeing, dressing, or spreading on a turkey or chicken before baking.

Try olive oil flavored with rosemary or fresh sage to baste on a turkey or chicken before roasting. Use grapeseed oil flavored with dill to sauté red snapper or salmon fish cakes. Try olive oil flavored with fresh basil lightly drizzled over your next homemade pizza, before baking. Chicken sautéed in olive oil flavored with fresh tarragon gives a wonderful flavor to the chicken. If you are adding garlic to the oil, it is best to soak the garlic in vinegar overnight, drain it, and then add it to the oil. Flavored oils are fun to experiment with and they look beautiful in clear fancy bottles to give as gifts.

© Burke/Triolo

JERKY

My boys love jerky. I usually make it only using flank steak, brisket, or eye of the round. You can also make it using lamb, pork, or game.

I partially freeze my meat because it makes it so much easier to slice it thinly. You then put the meat into a shallow container and pour on your sauce. Turn the meat so all slices are covered on all sides. Cover the dish tightly and refrigerate 6 to 12 hours, turning the meat occasionally. Blot the meat before you dry it to remove excess sauce, or the meat will take forever to dry.

If you use a dehydrator follow the manufacturer's directions. They usually tell you to start with a temperature of 140°F to 160°F, and then after 3 hours or so to turn it down to 130°F. If you use your oven start at 200°F and then turn it down to warm until it is dry. Place meat on the top rack of the oven and put cookie sheets on the bottom rack to catch the drippings. Blot the meat occasionally while it is drying. The drying process can take 6 to 12 hours. The jerky is done when it bends but does not break. Test a piece by cooling it first. To store the jerky, use a jar with a loose-fitting lid. I use a cookie jar. If you tightly wrap it, it will become moist and spoil. You can usually store it in a container with a loose fitting lid for 1 to 2 months. Good luck. In my house I'm lucky if it lasts a week, the kids love it so.

© Susanna Pashko/Envision

TERIYAKI JERKY

½ cup chicken broth

½ cup soy sauce

½ cup sherry

2 teaspoons sugar

2 teaspoons cornstarch

2 pounds brisket

Combine chicken broth, soy sauce, and sherry. Bring to a boil and add sugar. Stir to dissolve. Mix cornstarch with 2 tablespoons water and add to broth and cook until thickened. Remove from heat and cool. Partially freeze meat and slice thin. Put into a shallow pan and pour sauce over the meat. Turn all the meat to be sure it is covered with sauce. Cover tightly and refrigerate for 8 hours. Dab meat on a paper towel and dry in a dehydrator or an oven. Turn the dehydrator to 140°F, after a few hours turn it down to 130°F until it is dry. Blot the meat once in a while as it dries. The whole process should take 7 or 8 hours. If you are using the oven turn it to 200°F for an hour and then down to warm until meat is dry. Blot and turn once in a while. Store in a container with a loose-fitting lid.

PHILIP'S COWBOY JERKY

2 pounds lean brisket

¾ cup fancy ketchup

1 teaspoon garlic powder

1 tablespoon steak sauce

1½ teaspoons liquid smoke

1 teaspoon cracked pepper

2 tablespoons soy sauce

1 tablespoon Worcestershire sauce

Partially freeze brisket and slice. A small home slicer works really well. Put meat into a 9 x 13-inch pan. Mix the rest of the ingredients together and blend well. Pour sauce over meat and turn so that all meat is well covered with sauce. Cover dish and refrigerate for 12 hours, turning meat twice while it marinates. After 12 hours remove meat from pan and dab each piece with a paper towel. If you put the jerky in a dehydrator use a temperature of 140° to 170°F for the first 3 hours, then turn it down to 130° until it is dry. The drying process will take about 7 or 8 hours. If you do not have a dehydrator, use your oven. Set it at 200°F for the first 2 hours and then turn it to warm until it is dry. Occasionally blot the jerky with paper towels while it is drying. The drying process in the oven can take 8 to 10 hours. The jerky is done when the meat strips bend but do not break. Let jerky cool thoroughly and then store in a container with a loose-fitting lid.

T.J.'S BARBECUED JERKY

1½ pounds flank steak

¾ cup ketchup

¼ cup brown sugar

3 tablespoons soy sauce

1 tablespoon Worcestershire sauce

2 teaspoons molasses

1 tablespoon hoisin sauce

1 tablespoon honey

2 teaspoons liquid smoke

2 bay leaves, crushed

Partially freeze flank steak. Cut meat diagonally into very thin slices. Put meat into a pan with a tight-fitting lid. Pour sauce on meat and turn meat to coat all slices. Cover tightly and let marinate in the refrigerator for 8 to 12 hours. Occasionally mix meat so it all is covered equally with sauce. Remove meat and dab with paper towels. Put on top rack of a 200°F oven, if you don't have a dehydrator, and place a cookie sheet on bottom rack to catch drippings. After an hour or so, turn down to warm. Occasionally blot meat with a paper towel while it is drying. When dry (about 7 or 8 hours) and cool, store in a container with a loose-fitting lid.

BABY FOOD

I have made baby food with the strainer attachment that Cuisinarts have for their food processor. The food comes out beautifully pureed—equal to that sold by brand names in the stores.

Cook the food to a soft consistency and puree. If your baby is on junior foods your processor with the metal blade will do fine, but for younger babies the strainer is excellent.

I only show processing times for fruit-based baby food because proper processing times for pureed vegetables and meats have not yet been determined by the USDA. However, you can puree meats and vegetables and refrigerate them *to be used within two days.*

Fruits can be successfully canned and are processed for 25 minutes. I put the baby food in 4-ounce jars because of the convenient size.

Clean, peel, and seed fruit. Measure the fruit and add 1 cup of water for each pound of fruit you have. Cook until the fruit is very soft. Puree the fruit and taste. If you think it needs a little sugar add a teaspoon at a time. Remember, the baby does not need things sweet. But some fruits like apricots need their tartness diminished a little. It would be a good idea to ask your doctor about amounts of sugar and salt to add to the foods. Not much, I am sure.

Fruits suitable for baby food are apples, pears, plums, and peaches. You can also mix fruits or add a little orange juice to change the flavor a little.

If you want to make baby food from vegetables like beans, squash, or peas, just cook the vegetables in boiling water as usual. You can add a little salt to the water or eliminate it altogether. When the vegetables are tender, drain and puree them in the food processor. Add a little water (or chicken broth, if the baby is older) if the mixture is too thick. The USDA has not established a safe processing time so I would only make enough to refrigerate for a couple of days.

You can also cook chicken or beef in a little water until done. Puree this in the processor or the strainer and then thin with some of the cooking liquid. Again the USDA has not established a safe processing time for pureed meat so only make enough for a couple of days and keep refrigerated.

You cannot process baby food for the same length of time given for recipes of whole or sliced products, because pureed food is much denser and takes longer to arrive at the same internal temperature as sliced food. The processing time is the same for fruit, however, because of the acid content.

CHAPTER SEVEN

GIFTS FROM THE KITCHEN

Everyone loves to receive gifts from the kitchen; it gives those receiving them a special feeling knowing that you took the time to create something distinctive. In this chapter are some wonderful ideas for special, homemade treats, from Peach Brandy to Caramel Popcorn to Hot Dill Mustard. Of course, any recipe in this book will make a splendid gift. Place these goodies in beautiful canisters or bottles, for that extra-special touch.

All gifts that you are sending in a bottle or jar—or any other fragile container—must be packed very carefully so that they won't break. If you are shipping more than one bottle or jar in a box, be sure you allow ample room around each—at least three inches. Wrap each container in a layer of newspaper. It is a good idea to cover the bottom of these containers with shredded foam to absorb any shock. Always fill any empty spaces in the box with newspapers or foam. Always label the package as FRAGILE.

If you are shipping many different kinds of goodies in one box, wrap each one individually in plastic or foil. This way, if one breaks, the other will still be protected from absorbing the liquid or odors.

BARBECUE SAUCE

44 ounces ketchup

½ cup brown sugar

½ cup honey

⅓ cup cider vinegar

¼ cup molasses

3 tablespoons Worcestershire sauce

3 bay leaves, crushed

2 teaspoons liquid smoke

1 teaspoon cracked pepper

1 teaspoon salt

1 small can (8¾ ounces) crushed pineapple

2 cloves garlic, minced

½ cup soy sauce

1 teaspoon ginger

Combine all ingredients in a large saucepan. Cook, stirring occasionally, 30 to 40 minutes until sauce is well blended. Ladle into hot jars. Clean rims of jars and seal. Process in a water bath canner for 20 minutes.

Makes 7 pints.

© Steven Mark Needham/Envision

APPLE SYRUP

1 pound apples, peeled and
   sliced

1 teaspoon cinnamon

½ teaspoon nutmeg

2 tablespoons bottled
   lemon juice

¼ cup (½ stick) unsalted
   butter

1 cup brown sugar

1 teaspoon vanilla

1 cup water

1 tablespoon Grand Marnier

1 tablespoon plus 1 teaspoon
   cornstarch

Put apples in a pan with a lid. Add cinnamon, nutmeg, lemon juice, and butter. Cover and cook apples over medium heat until soft. Use the strainer attachment for the Cuisinart if you have one, otherwise use a blender or food processor to puree the apples. Put the pureed apples back into the pan and add the rest of the ingredients except the cornstarch. Stir constantly until sugar is dissolved and the mixture begins to boil. Boil for 3 to 5 mintues. Mix the cornstarch with ¼ cup water until it is dissolved, then stir it into the syrup mixture and cook until it slightly thickens. Pour into a bottle or jar with a tight-fitting lid and keep in the refrigerator for up to a month. This is great on French toast, pancakes, or waffles.

Makes 2 cups of syrup.

PEACH BRANDY

1 gallon vodka

4 pounds peaches (about
   8 large)

1 to 1½ pounds clear rock
   candy

Place vodka in a large glass container with a tight-fitting lid. Add 2 pounds of peaches, peeled and sliced. Add the rock candy. In about a month the peaches will lose their color. Remove those peaches and peel and slice 2 more pounds of peaches. Add to vodka. Shake bottle several times and if the vodka flavor is still too strong add ¼ to ½ pound more rock candy. Shake container every month and let mixture stay in a dark, cool place for 3 to 5 months. Strain the brandy and put it in pretty bottles with tight-fitting caps or corks.

CARAMEL SAUCE

This is a great sauce. If you want to thin it to spread on a dessert plate and set a piece of fresh baked apple pie on, just warm it with a couple tablespoons of cream. When this sauce is refrigerated it gets very thick. To use, just put in the microwave for 30 seconds or let come to room temperature.

1 cup (2 sticks) unsalted butter

½ cup evaporated milk

1 teaspoon vanilla

½ cup light corn syrup

1 teaspoon salt

Melt butter, add rest of ingredients, and mix well. Bring to a boil, stirring constantly, then let boil 3 minutes without stirring. Remove from heat and ladle into hot half-pint jars. Seal and let cool. When cool, refrigerate. This sauce will stay good for 3 to 4 weeks.

Makes 3 half-pints.

© Steven Mark Needham/Envision

HOT DILL MUSTARD

½ cup dry mustard

1 cup cider vinegar

2 tablespoons mustard seed

1 cup champagne

¼ cup brown sugar

1 teaspoon lemon pepper

1½ teaspoons salt

1 tablespoon dried dill

3 egg yolks

Mix dry mustard, vinegar, mustard seed, and champagne together. Let sit 2 to 3 hours. Add brown sugar, lemon pepper, salt, and dill. Mix well and put in the top of a double boiler. Warm over medium heat, stirring constantly. Beat egg yolks with a fork and add a couple tablespoons of the warm mustard. Blend yolk mixture into mustard and continue cooking until mustard begins to thicken. Ladle into jars with tight-fitting corks or lids. Can be refrigerated for 1 to 2 months.

Makes 2½ cups of mustard.

© Steven Mark Needham/Envision

SUZY'S CARAMEL POPCORN

This caramel corn is delicious. If stored in an airtight container it will last nicely for 2 weeks. If a store in your area carries Land O Lakes® unsalted butter, please use it for this recipe. Another hint comes after the sauce has cooked for 5 minutes. You then add the baking soda and vanilla at once and stir vigorously for about 2 minutes. The sauce will lighten in color and double in size. If you just stir it you will have crystallized sugar corn. If you do it right you will have shiny, crunchy caramel corn.

1 cup (2 sticks) unsalted butter

2 cups light brown sugar

½ cup light corn syrup

½ teaspoon salt

½ teaspoon baking soda

1 teaspoon vanilla

6 quarts popped popcorn

Melt butter in a heavy pan. Add sugar, syrup, and salt. Bring to a boil, stirring constantly. When it begins to boil stop stirring and let cook at medium heat for 5 minutes. Remove from heat and immediately add baking soda and vanilla all at once. Stir vigorously for 2 minutes or until caramel doubles in size. Put popcorn in a large roasting pan and pour hot caramel sauce over. Fold caramel and popcorn and cook in a 250°F oven for 50 minutes. Stir popcorn every 15 minutes to distribute caramel evenly. Remove popcorn and spread on a wooden surface or on a large cookie sheet. Separate with two spoons and let cool completely. Store in an airtight container.

Makes 6 quarts.

COCKTAIL PINE NUTS

½ cup (1 stick) unsalted butter

¾ teaspoon garlic salt

⅓ cup grated Parmesan cheese

¼ teaspoon white pepper

⅛ teaspoon cayenne

½ teaspoon celery seed

6 drops hot pepper sauce

½ teaspoon minced parsley

1 pound pine nuts

Melt butter, stir in cheese and all the spices. Put the pine nuts in a pie dish and pour the butter sauce over the nuts. Mix well. Put into a 300°F oven for 20 to 25 minutes, stirring frequently. Remove the nuts and let them cool on a cookie sheet lined with paper towels. Store in a jar or can with a tight-fitting lid. Use within a week.

CINDY'S GRANOLA

8 cups rolled oats

3 cups raw peanuts

2 cups unsalted sunflower seeds

1 cup almonds

1½ cups unsalted pumpkin seeds

1 package (7 ounces) unsweetened coconut

1 cup (2 sticks) butter

¾ cup honey

1 teaspoon vanilla

¾ cup brown sugar

½ teaspoon nutmeg

1½ teaspoons cinnamon

1 teaspoon salt

½ pound raisins

½ pound dried apricots, diced

Put oats, peanuts, sunflower seeds, almonds, pumpkin seeds, and coconut into a large, deep baking or roasting pan, and mix well. Melt butter, and mix in honey and vanilla. Sprinkle the brown sugar, nutmeg, cinnamon, and salt over the oat mixture. Mix well. Pour the butter mixture over the spiced oat mixture and stir to blend well. Put into a 250°F oven for 25 minutes, stirring every 10 minutes to blend well. Add raisins and dried apricots and cook for 5 more minutes. Spread out on a large cookie sheet to cool. Store in jars with tight-fitting lids.

Makes 4 quarts of granola.

KITCHEN METRICS

For cooking and baking convenience, use the following metric measurements:

SPOONS:

1/4 teaspoon = 1 milliliter
1/2 teaspoon = 2 milliliters
1 teaspoon = 5 milliliters
1 tablespoon = 15 milliliters
2 tablespoons = 25 milliliters
3 tablespoons = 50 milliliters

CUPS:

1/4 cup = 50 milliliters
1/3 cup = 75 milliliters
1/2 cup = 125 milliliters
2/3 cup = 150 milliliters
3/4 cup = 175 milliliters
1 cup = 250 milliliters

OVEN TEMPERATURES:

200° F = 100° C
225° F = 110° C
250° F = 120° C
275° F = 140° C
300° F = 150° C
325° F = 160° C
350° F = 180° C
375° F = 190° C
400° F = 200° C
425° F = 220° C
450° F = 230° C
475° F = 240° C

WEIGHT AND MEASURE EQUIVALENTS

1 inch = 2.54 centimeters
1 square inch = 6.45 square centimeters
1 foot = .3048 meters
1 square foot = 929.03 square centimeters
1 yard = .9144 meters
1 square yard = .84 square meters
1 ounce = 28.35 grams
1 pound = 453.59 grams

SHOPPING GUIDE

The Crate and Barrel
190 Northfield Road
Northfield, IL 60093

Cuisinart
120 Top Gallant Road
Stamford, CT 06912-006
Strainer attachment

The Chefs Catalogue
3915 Commerical
Northbrook, IL 60062

Glashaus, Inc.
415 W. Golf Road
Suite 13
Arlington Heights, IL 60005
Rubber rings

Sears, Roebuck and Co.
Telecatalog Center
9390 Bunsen Parkway
Louisville, KY 40220
Nice pressure canners

William Glen
Mail-Order Department
2651 El Paseo Lane
Sacramento, CA 95821

Williams-Sonoma
Mail-Order Department
P.O. Box 7456
San Francisco, CA 94120

Courtesy Ball Jar Corporation

INDEX

A

Apples
  butter, 81
  mint jelly, 60
  and pear chutney, 107
  and pear preserves, 74
  pie filling, 46
  and plum butter, 81
  and plum conserves, 78
  preparation of, 35
  spiced no-sugar jelly, 68
  syrup, 121
Applesauce, 35, 38
Apricots, 38
  butter, 80
  and pineapple jam, 66
  preparation of, 35
Artichokes, preparation of, 86
Asparagus, 90
  preparation of, 86
Aunt Rose's Relish, 104

B

Baby food, 116
Barbecued jerky, 115
Barbecue sauce, 120
Basil vinegar, 112
Basil tomato sauce, 51
Beans, pickled, 102
Beets
  pickled, 102
  preparation of, 86
Berries
  preparation of, 35
  See also specific berries
Betty Keech's Dill Pickles, 101
Blackberry vinegar, 110
Blueberries
  and cherry conserves, 78
  and cherry jam, 66
  pie filling, 46
Botulism, 21
Brandied Cherries, 39
Brandy, peach, 121
Bread and Butter Pickles, 100

C

Canned Tomatoes, 51
Canning
  appropriate foods for, 13-14
  cooling, testing, and storing, 21
  equipment for, 14-18
  of fruit, 24-25
  fruit preparation methods, 35-37
  microwave, 19
  preparation methods, 19
  procedures for vegetables, 85
  questions about, 34
  sealing methods, 20
  spoilage, 21
  of tomatoes, 26-33
Caramel popcorn, 123
Caramel sauce, 121
Carrie's Favorite Apple Butter, 81
Carrots
  with mint, 93
  pickled, 102
  preparation of, 87
  and string beans, 90
Celery, preparation of, 87
Cherries
  and blueberry conserves, 78
  and blueberry jam, 66
  brandied, 39
  pie filling, 49
  preparation of, 35
  preserves, 75
Chunky Applesauce, 38
Chutney
  apple-pear, 107
  mango, 107
  peachy ginger, 107
  processing, 98
  Rusty's, 107
Cindy's Granola, 123
Cinnamon Pears, 42
Cocktail pine nuts, 123
Conserves, 55, 78-79
  cherry-blueberry, 78
  fig, 78
  lemon-cranberry, 79
  methods for, 56
  plum-apple, 78
Cooling, 21

Corn
  preparation of, 87
  relish, 105
Cranberries and lemon conserves, 79
Creme de Menthe pears, 42
Currant jelly, 60

D

Dill
  mustard, 122
  pickles, 101
  vinegar, 111
Dilly Beans, 102

E

Equipment, 14-18, 70, 84

F

Fancy Ketchup, 52
Figs
  conserves, 78
  preparation method for, 35
Food spoilage, 21
Freezer jams, 69
Fresh Basil Tomato Sauce, 51
Fruit
  canning procedures, 24-25
  preparation methods, 35-37
  questions about canning, 34
Fruit butters, 55, 80-81
  apple, 81
  apricot, 80
  loquat, 80
  plum-apple, 81
Fruit cocktail, 40
Fruit juices, preparation of, 35

G

Ginger chutney, 107
Gooseberry preserves, 75
Granola, 123
Grapefruit
  marmalade, 76
  preparation of, 36
Grapes
  no-sugar jelly, 68
  preparation of, 36
Green Beans Tied with Carrots, 90
Green relish, 105
Greens, preparation of, 87

H
Hot Dill Mustard, 122

J
Jams, 55, 62-68
apricot-pineapple, 66
cherry-blueberry, 66
low-sugar cooking, 67
low-sugar plum-peach, 68
methods for, 56
no-cook (freezer), 69
no-cook peach, 69
no-sugar peach, 68
peach, 64
peach-raspberry, 64
problems with, 58
rhubarb-peach, 65
strawberry no-cook, 69
Jars, 14-15
Jellies, 56
currant, 60
low-sugar cooking, 67
methods for, 58
mint apple, 60
no-sugar grape, 68
pepper, 61
pomegranate, 60
problems with, 58
spiced no-sugar apple, 68
white zinfandel, 60
Jerky
barbecued, 115
Philip's Cowboy, 115
teriyaki, 115

K
Ketchup, 52

L
Lemon
and cranberry conserves, 79
and thyme vinegar, 110
Lids, 14-15, 20
Lima beans, preparation of, 86
Lime marmalade, 76
Loquats, 40
butter, 80
Low-acid foods, botulism and, 21
Low-Sugar Plum-Peach Jam with Pectin, 68

M
Mango chutney, 107
Marmalades, 56, 76-77
lime, 76
methods for, 56
orange-pineapple, 77
pink grapefruit, 76
Mary's Sweet Pickles, 100
Melange of Peppers, 92
Michelle's Pickled Carrots, 102
Microwave canning, 19
Mint, carrots with, 93
Mint Apple Jelly, 60
Mixed Fruit Cocktail, 40
Mixed Vegetables, 90
Mushrooms, preparation of, 87
Mustard, hot dill, 122

N
Nectarines, preparation of, 36
No-Sugar Apple Jelly, 68
No-Sugar Grape Jelly, 68
No-Sugar Peach Jam with Pectin, 68

O
Oils, flavored, 113
Okra, preparation of, 87
Onions, preparation of, 88
Oranges
and pineapple marmalade, 77
preparation of, 36

P
Peaches
brandy, 121
ginger chutney, 107
jam, 64
no-cook jam, 69
no-sugar jam, 68
in peach wine, 41
pie filling, 49
and pineapple preserves, 72
and plum low-sugar jam, 68
preparation of, 36
preserves, 72
and raspberry jam, 64
and rhubarb jam, 65
and strawberry preserves, 72
Peachy Ginger Chutney, 107

Pears
and apple chutney, 107
and apple preserves, 74
cinnamon, 42
creme de menthe, 42
preparation of, 37
raspberries and, 42
and rhubarb pie filling, 48
Peas, preparation of, 88
Pectin
low-sugar plum-peach jam with, 68
no-sugar peach jam with, 68
Peppers
jelly, 61
melange of, 92
preparation of, 88
relish, 104
Philip's Cowboy Jerky, 115
Pickles
beans, 102
beets, 102
bread and butter, 100
carrots, 102
dill, 101
equipment for, 96
ingredients for pickling, 96
problems with, 99
processing, 98
rules, 98
sweet, 100
sweet chips, 100
types, 95-96
zucchini, 102
Pie fillings, 44-49
apple, 46
blueberry, 46
cherry, 49
peach, 49
rhubarb and pear, 48
Pineapple
and apricot jam, 66
and orange marmalade, 77
and peach preserves, 72
preparation of, 37
Pine nuts, 123
Pink Grapefruit Marmalade, 76
Pizza Sauce, 52
Plums
and apple butter, 81

and apple conserves, 78
and peach low-sugar jam, 68
preparation of, 37
Pomegranate Jelly, 60
Popcorn, caramel, 123
Potatoes, preparation of, 88
Preparation methods, 19
Preserves, 56
    apple-pear, 74
    cherry, 75
    equipment for, 70
    gooseberry, 75
    methods for, 56
    peach, 72
    peach-pineapple, 72
    strawberry, 75
    strawberry-peach, 72
Prunes
    preparation of, 37
    stewed, 43
Pumpkin, preparation of, 88, 89

R
Raspberries
    and peach jam, 64
    pears and, 42
    vinegar, 112
Relish
    Aunt Rose's, 104
    corn, 105
    green, 105
    pepper, 104
    processing, 98
Rhubarb
    and peach jam, 65
    and pear pie filling, 48
    preparation method for, 37
Rusty's Chutney, 107

S
Safety, botulism and, 21
Salsa, 52
Sauces
    barbecue, 120
    basil tomato, 51
    caramel, 121
    ketchup, 52
    pizza, 52

salsa, 52
tomato, 52
Sealing methods, 20
Spiced No-Sugar Apple Jelly, 68
Spiced Peaches in Peach Wine, 41
Spoilage, 21
Squash, preparation of, 88, 89
Stewed Prunes, 43
Storage, 21
Strawberries
    no-cook jam, 69
    and peach preserves, 72
    preparation of, 37
    preserves, 75
String beans
    and carrots, 90
    pickled, 102
    preparation of, 86
Sugar, reduction of, 67
Suzy's Caramel Popcorn, 123
Sweet Chips, 100
Sweet pickles, 100
Sweet potatoes, preparation of, 88
Syrup, apple, 121

T
Tarragon vinegar, 110
Teriyaki jerky, 115
Testing, 21
Thyme and lemon vinegar, 110
T.J.'s Barbecued Jerky, 115
Tomatoes, 50-52
    canned, 51
    canning procedures for, 26-33
    ketchup, 52
    pizza sauce, 52
    preparation of, 37
    questions about canning, 34
    salsa, 52
    sauce, 51, 52
Tomato juice, preparation of, 37
Turnips, preparation of, 89

U
USDA Apple Pie Filling, 46
USDA Cherry Pie Filling, 49

V
Vegetables
    mixed, 90
    preparation of, 86-89
    pressure canner for, 84
    problems with, 85
    procedures for, 85
    processing times for, 84
Vinegars
    basil, 112
    blueberry, 110
    dill, 111
    lemon-thyme, 110
    raspberry, 112
    tarragon, 110

W
White Zinfandel Jelly, 60
Wilma's Green Relish, 106
Wine, peaches in, 41

Z
Zinfandel jelly, 60
Zucchini pickles, 102